THE
BEATLES
ILLUSTRATED
LYRICS 1

Julian Allen
Clive Arrowsmith
David Bailey
Stephen Bobroff
Mel Calman
Seymour Chwast
John Deakin
Erté
John Farman
Hans Feurer
Folon
Milton Glaser
John Glashan
Rick Griffin
Robert Grossman
Chadwick Hall
Rudolf Hausner
David Hockney
Art Kane
David King

THE BEATLES ILLUSTRATED LYRICS 1

Edited by Alan Aldridge

Roger Law
Peter Le Vasseur
James Lloyd
Jean Loup Sieff
Brian Love
Peter Max
James Marsh
Mike McInnerney
David Montgomery
Phillipe Mora
Victor Moscoso
Stanley Mouse
Ronald Searle
Donald Silverstein
Diane Tipple
Harri Peccinotti
Colette Portal
Enzo Ragazzini
Ethan Russell
Justin Todd
Roland Topor
Tomi Ungerer
Richard Weigand
Harry Willock

Delta/Seymour Lawrence

A DELTA/SEYMOUR LAWRENCE BOOK

Published by
Dell Publishing Co., Inc.
1 Dag Hammarskjold Plaza
New York, New York 10017

First published in Great Britain in 1969 by Macdonald Unit 75,
London

Delta ® TM 755118, Dell Publishing Co., Inc.

ISBN: 0-440-50503-8

Reprinted by arrangement with Delacorte Press/
Seymour Lawrence

Printed in the United States of America
First Delta printing—September 1980

Dedicated to

who didn't see it and to
Rita, Miles and Saffron who did.

I'd love to turn you on

Overleaf: Alan Aldridge explains how this book of The Beatles' Illustrated Lyrics came about.

Illustration from article 'Beatles Sinister Songbook' – The Observer November 1967

It is almost irreverent and certainly irrelevant to think of the Beatles in mundane terms as the pop group who became the biggest rock and roll attraction ever. While their early appearances caused unprecedented scenes of mass hysteria, their music has developed into a fascinating social history of our generation and its culture. It was the realisation of the elevation of pop music and allied pop culture by the Beatles which drew my interest to the possibility of producing this book.

I first became aware of the depth of the lyrics to the Beatles' songs when I went to a party in 1967 during the Sergeant Pepper era. Someone whispered in my ear that Lucy in the Sky with Diamonds was a song about an LSD trip. Although ambiguity in the lyrics to popular music was no new thing, the scale of the various interpretations of the songs on the Sergeant Pepper album so intrigued me that I began reading *all* the lyrics of Beatles' songs and finding, or imagining, all kinds of hidden meanings. One phrase in particular staggered me: "keeping her face in a jar by the door", from Eleanor Rigby. This seemed to me pure surrealism. And as this was an area in which I was working in illustrations, I decided in my complete naivety that I should interview the author of the line, Paul McCartney. The result was an article, which when published with my own illustrations, created a deluge of fan mail. It led me directly to begin planning this book of the best Beatles' lyrics.

Altogether something like 180 songs by the Beatles have been published, but since many of the earlier compositions are very repetitive in theme and would not have provided enough difference in illustration, we were able to weed them out. Having done this we sent lists to the 43 contributors and asked them to tick off the ones they wanted to do. Ironically enough it quickly got to the stage where nearly all the ones *I* wanted to do had been chosen by someone else–but never mind!

What I have tried to do is to present a book which is as entertaining to the eye and the imagination as a Beatles album is to the ear. For an artist it is a challenging exercise to take a lyric and illustrate it. And of course, there is a very long tradition of this. Artists have always illustrated passages from the Bible or from poems, and we have tried to do the same thing here. In a sense, the

Beatles are a religion: they turn people on by what they say and by what they represent.

For me, the music and lyrics of the Beatles are a tremendous springboard into the imagination. No matter how good or how bad their poetry may be, it is universal in appeal and being so is that much more viable a thing to illustrate.

The lyrics are the catalyst for the artists' imaginations. Some of the illustrations here are very imaginative: others seem straightforward. But maybe that is because I have not caught their meanings first time. I am always staggered for example, at the number of people who listen to Hey Jude without understanding it. But I must admit that although I have read all the lyrics very carefully many times, I cannot honestly claim to understand them fully yet. I should like to believe that this book is more than merely a selection of drawings of Beatles' songs. I see it as an illustration of the sixties.

For the section on fan art we advertised widely. Treasured drawings were sent to us in masses. They ranged from 6′ 6″ canvases right down to little pencilled drawings of John and Yoko. We also received large numbers of abusive letters . . . something which was new to me. I suppose when there is a lot of loving directed at something or someone, then there must be a lot of hating too.

The Beatles and their music have captured the tempo of the world today. I believe that the illustrations in this book may illuminate their contribution to the style of their generation.

Alan Aldridge, 1969

'There's a lot of random in our songs ...
writing, thinking,
letting others think of bits –
then bang, you have the jigsaw puzzle' - Paul

Mother nature's son

Born a poor young country boy –
Mother Nature's son.
All day long I'm sitting singing songs
for everyone.
Sit beside a mountain stream – see
her waters rise.
Listen to the pretty sound of music as
she flies.
Find me in my field of grass – Mother
Nature's son.
Swaying daisies sing a lazy song
beneath the sun.
Mother Nature's son.

**''I've never really done anything to
create what has happened. It creates
itself. I'm here because it happened.
But I didn't do anything to make it
happen apart from saying 'Yes'.'' –
Ringo**

Good day sunshine

Good day sunshine, good day sunshine,
good day sunshine.
I need to laugh, and when the sun is out,
I've got something I can laugh about.
I feel good in a special way,
I'm in love, and it's a sunny day.
Good day sunshine, good day sunshine,
good day sunshine.
We take a walk, the sun is shining down,
burns my feet as they touch the ground.
Good day sunshine, good day sunshine,
good day sunshine.
And then we lie beneath a shady tree,
I love her and she's loving me.
She feels good, she knows she's looking
fine,
I'm so proud to know that she is mine.
Good day sunshine, good day sunshine,
good day sunshine.
Good day sunshine, good day sunshine.

**''Don't forget to say I was wearing a
very big smile'' – Linda Eastman to
reporters after her marriage to Paul**

All I've got to do

Whenever I want you around, yeh,
All I gotta do
Is call you on the phone and you'll come
running home,
Yeh, that's all I gotta do.
And when I wanna kiss you, yeh,
All I gotta do
Is whisper in your ear the words you want
to hear,
And I'll be kissing you.
And the same goes for me whenever you
want me at all,
I'll be here, yes I will, whenever you call,
You just gotta call on me, yeh, you just
gotta call on me.
And when I wanna kiss you, yeh,
All I gotta do
Is call you on the phone and you'll come
running home,
Yeh, that's all I gotta do.
And the same goes for me whenever you
want me at all,
I'll be here, yes I will, whenever you call,
You just gotta call on me, yeh, you just
gotta call on me.

Ob-la-di, Ob-la-da

Desmond has a barrow in the market
place.
Molly is a singer in a band.
Desmond says to Molly – girl I like your
face
And Molly says this as she takes him by
The hand.
Obladi oblada life goes on bra
Lala how the life goes on
Obladi oblada life goes on bra
Lala how the life goes on.
Desmond takes a trolley to the jewellers
stores,
Buys a twenty carat golden ring.
Takes it back to Molly waiting at the door
And as he gives it to her she begins to
Sing.
In a couple of years they have built
A home sweet home
With a couple of kids running in the yard
Of Desmond and Molly Jones.
Happy ever after in the market place
Desmond lets the children lend a hand.
Molly stays at home and does her pretty
face
And in the evening she still sings it with
The band.
Happy ever after in the market place
Molly lets the children lend a hand.
Desmond stays at home and does his
pretty face
And in the evening she's a singer with the
Band.
And if you want some fun – take Obladi
Oblada.

Michelle

Michelle ma belle
These are words that go together well, my
Michelle,
Michelle ma belle,
Sont les mots qui vont tres bien ensemble
tres bien ensemble.
I love you, I love you, I love you,
That's all I want to say,
Until I find a way,
I will say the only words I know that
you'll understand.
Michelle ma belle,
Sont les mots qui vont tres bien ensemble
tres bien ensemble.
I need to, I need to, I need to,
I need to make you see,
oh what you mean to me,
Until I do I'm hoping you will know what
I mean.
I love you.
I want you, I want you, I want you,
I think you know by now,
I'll get to you somehow,
Until I do I'm telling you so you'll
understand.
Michelle ma belle,
Sont les mots qui vont tres bien ensemble
tres bien ensemble.
I will say the only words I know that
you'll understand,
my Michelle.

"While we were in India they were all making their plans and I was going to produce Yoko and I would've been producing her had we not fallen in love anyway. But it didn't turn out like that. And now we're together. Yes, it turned out much better, and it's getting better all the time . . ."

Getting better

It's getting better all the time
I used to get mad at my school
the teachers who taught me weren't cool
Holding me down, turning me round
filling me up with your rules.
I've got to admit it's getting better
It's a little better all the time
I have to admit it's getting better
it's getting better since you've been mine.
Me used to be angry young man
me hiding me head in the sand
You gave me the word
I finally heard
I'm doing the best that I can.
I admit it's getting better
It's a little better all the time yes
I admit it's getting better
it's getting better since you've been mine.
I used to be cruel to my woman
I beat her and kept her apart from the things that she loved
Man I was mean but I'm changing my scene
and I'm doing the best that I can.
I admit it's getting better
a little better all the time
yes I admit it's getting better
it's getting better since you've been mine.
Getting so much better all the time.

Helter skelter

When I get to the bottom I go back to the top of the slide.
Where I stop and I turn and I go for a ride
Till I get to the bottom and I see you again.
Do you, don't you want me to love you.
I'm coming down fast but I'm miles above you.
Tell me tell me tell me come on tell me the answer.
You may be a lover but you ain't no dancer.
Helter skelter helter skelter
Helter skelter.
Will you, won't you want me to make you.
I'm coming down fast but don't let me break you.
Tell me tell me tell me the answer.
You may be a lover but you ain't no dancer.
Look out helter skelter helter skelter
Helter skelter
Look out, cause here she comes.
When I get to the bottom I go back to the top of the slide
And I stop and I turn and I go for a ride
And I get to the bottom and I see you again.
Well do you, don't you want me to make you.
I'm coming down fast but don't let me break you.
Tell me tell me tell me the answer.
You may be a lover but you ain't no dancer.
Look out helter skelter helter skelter
Helter skelter
Look out helter skelter
She's coming down fast
Yes she is
Yes she is.

I'm so tired.

I'm so tired

I'm so tired, I haven't slept a wink,
I'm so tired, my mind is on the blink.
I wonder should I get up and fix myself a
drink.
No, no, no.
I'm so tired I don't know what to do.
I'm so tired my mind is set on you.
I wonder should I call you but I know
what you'd do.
You'd say I'm putting you on.
But it's no joke, it's doing me harm.
You know I can't sleep, I can't stop my
brain
You know it's three weeks, I'm going
insane.
You know I'd give you everything I've got
for a little peace of mind.
I'm so tired, I'm feeling so upset
Although I'm so tired I'll have another
cigarette
And curse Sir Walter Raleigh.
He was such a stupid git.

**"Touring was murder. We hardly
saw any of America because we had
to stay inside hotel rooms all the
time. And we were always dead
beat" – Ringo**

The word

Say the word and you'll be free,
Say the word and be like me,
Say the word I'm thinking of,
Have you heard the word is love.
It's so fine, it's sunshine,
It's the word love.
In the beginning I misunderstood,
But now I've got it the word is good.
Say the word and you'll be free,
Say the word and be like me,
Say the word I'm thinking of,
Have you heard the word is love.
It's so fine, it's sunshine,
It's the word love.
Everywhere I go I hear it said,
In the good and the bad books that I have read.
Say the word and you'll be free,
Say the word and be like me
Say the word I'm thinking of
Have you heard the word is love.
It's so fine, it's sunshine,
It's the word love.
Now that I know what I feel must be right,
I mean to show ev'rybody the light,
Give the word a chance to say,
That the word is just the way,
It's the word I'm thinking of,
And the only word is love.
It's so fine it's sunshine,
It's the word love.
Say the word love,
Say the word love,
Say the word love,
Say the word love.

Drive my car

Asked a girl what she wanted to be,
she said, baby can't you see?
I wanna be famous, a star of the screen,
but you can do something in between.
Baby, you can drive my car, yes I'm gonna be a star,
baby, you can drive my car, and maybe I'll love you.
I told that girl that my prospects were good,
she said, baby it's understood,
working for peanuts is all very fine,
but I can show you a better time.
Baby, you can drive my car, yes I'm gonna be a star,
baby, you can drive my car, and maybe I'll love you
Beep beep mm, beep beep yeh!
Baby, you can drive my car, yes I'm gonna be a star,
baby, you can drive my car, and maybe I'll love you.
I told that girl I could start right away,
and she said, listen, Babe, I've got something to say,
got no car, and it's breaking my heart,
but I've found a driver, that's a start.
Baby, you can drive my car, yes I'm gonna be a star,
baby, you can drive my car, and maybe I'll love you.
Beep beep mm, beep beep yeh!

The word "John and I would like to do songs with just one note like 'Long Tall Sally'. We get near it in 'The word.' The word is love.''—Paul

Drive my car "The truth is, I'm not a car addict. I feel embarrassed having to go into a garage and then pointing vaguely at the car and saying er, I think it's the, er, you know, er, that's gone wrong . . . '' – Paul

When I'm sixty-four

When I get older losing my hair,
many years from now.
Will you still be sending me a Valentine
birthday greetings bottle of wine.

If I'd been out till quarter to three
would you lock the door.
Will you still need me, will you still feed
me,
when I'm sixty four.
You'll be older too,

25

and if you say the word,
I could stay with you.
I could be handy, mending a fuse
when your lights have gone.
You can knit a sweater by the fireside
Sunday morning go for a ride,

doing the garden, digging the weeds,
who could ask for more.
Will you still need me, will you still feed me,
when I'm sixty-four.
Every summer we can rent a cottage,

27

in the Isle of Wight, if it's not too dear
we shall scrimp and save
grandchildren on your knee
Vera Chuck& Dave
send me a postcard, drop me a line,
stating point of view

indicate precisely what you mean to say
yours sincerely, wasting away
give me your answer, fill in a form
mine for evermore.
Will you still need me, will you still feed me.
When I'm sixty-four.

A day in the life

I read the news today oh boy
about a lucky man who made the grade
and though the news was rather sad
well I just had to laugh
I saw the photograph
He blew his mind out in a car
he didn't notice that the lights had
changed
a crowd of people stood and stared
they'd seen his face before
nobody was really sure
if he was from the House of Lords.
I saw a film today oh boy
the English Army had just won the war
a crowd of people turned away
but I just had to look
having read the book.
I'd love to turn you on
Woke up, got out of bed,
dragged a comb across my head
found my way downstairs and drank a
cup,
and looking up I noticed I was late.
Found my coat and grabbed my hat
made the bus in seconds flat
found my way upstairs and had a smoke,
and somebody spoke and I went into a
dream
I heard the news today oh boy
four thousand holes in Blackburn,
Lancashire
and though the holes were rather small
they had to count them all
now they know how many holes it takes
to fill the Albert Hall.
I'd love to turn you on.

"I was writing the song with the Daily Mail propped up in front of me on the piano, I had it open at their News In Brief, or Far or Near, whatever they call it. There was a paragraph about 4,000 holes in Blackburn, Lancashire, being discovered and there was still one word missing in that verse when we came to record. I knew the line had to go 'Now they know how many holes it takes to fill the Albert Hall.' It was a nonsense verse really, but for some reason I couldn't think of the verb. What did the holes do to the Albert Hall? It was Terry (Doran) who said 'fill' the Albert Hall.'' – John

Happiness is a warm gun

She's not a girl who misses much.
Do do do do do do do do
She's well acquainted with the touch of
the velvet hand
Like a lizard on a window pane.
The man in the crowd with the
multicoloured mirrors
On his hobnail boots
Lying with his eyes while his hands are
busy
Working overtime
A soap impression of his wife which he ate
And donated to the National Trust.
I need a fix 'cause I'm going down.
Down to the bits that I left uptown.
I need a fix 'cause I'm going down.
Mother Superior jump the gun
Mother Superior jump the gun
Mother Superior jump the gun
Mother Superior jump the gun.
Happiness is a warm gun
Happiness is a warm gun
When I hold you in my arms
And I feel my finger on your trigger
I know no one can do me no harm
because happiness is a warm gun.
Yes it is.

**"I think this is my favourite on
The Beatles album." – Paul**

In my life

There are places I'll remember
all my life, though some have changed,
some forever, not for better,
some have gone and some remain.
All these places had their moments,
with lovers and friends I still can recall,
some are dead and some are living,
in my life I've loved them all.
But of all these friends and lovers,
there is no one compared with you,
and these mem'ries lose their meaning
when I think of love as something new.
Though I know I'll never lose affection
for people and things that went before,
I know I'll often stop and think about
them,
in my life I'll love you more.
Though I know I'll never lose affection
for people and things that went before,
I know I'll often stop and think about
them
in my life I'll love you more.
In my life I'll love you more.

**"There is one thing I used to regret
and feel guilty about. When Ringo
joined us I used to act all big time with
him because I'd been in the business a
bit longer and felt superior. I was a
know-all. I'd been in the sixth form
and thought I'd read a bit, you know.
I began putting him off me, and me
off me." – Paul**

Peter Le Vasseur 1969

The continuing story of Bungalow Bill

Hey, Bungalow Bill
what did you kill
Bungalow Bill?
He went out tiger hunting with his
elephant and gun.
In case of accidents he always took his
mom.
He's the all American bullet-headed
saxon mother's son.
All the children sing
Hey, Bungalow Bill
What did you kill
Bungalow Bill?
Deep in the jungle where the mighty tiger
lies
Bill and his elephants were taken by
surprise.
So Captain Marvel zapped in right
between the eyes.
All the children sing
Hey, Bungalow Bill
What did you kill
Bungalow Bill?
The children asked him if to kill was not a
sin.
Not when he looked so fierce, his mother
butted in.
If looks could kill it would have been us
instead of him.
All the children sing
Hey, Bungalow Bill
What did you kill
Bungalow Bill?

"Lots of people who complained about us receiving the MBE received theirs for heroism in the war – for killing people. We received ours for entertaining other people. I'd say we deserve ours more. Wouldn't you?" – John

Martha my dear

Martha my dear though I spend my days
in conversation
Please
Remember me   Martha my love
Don't forget me   Martha my dear
Hold your head up you silly girl look what
you've done
When you find yourself in the thick of it
Help yourself to a bit of what is all
around you
Silly Girl.
Take a good look around you
Take a good look you're bound to see
That you and me were meant to be for
each other
Silly girl.
Hold your hand out you silly girl see what
you've done
When you find yourself in the thick of it
Help yourself to a bit of what is all around
you
Silly girl.
Martha my dear you have always been
my inspiration
Please
Be good to me   Martha my love
Don't forget me   Martha my dear.

"We had to buy a house in the country. We lived in town when Zak was a baby but we were always terrified that some

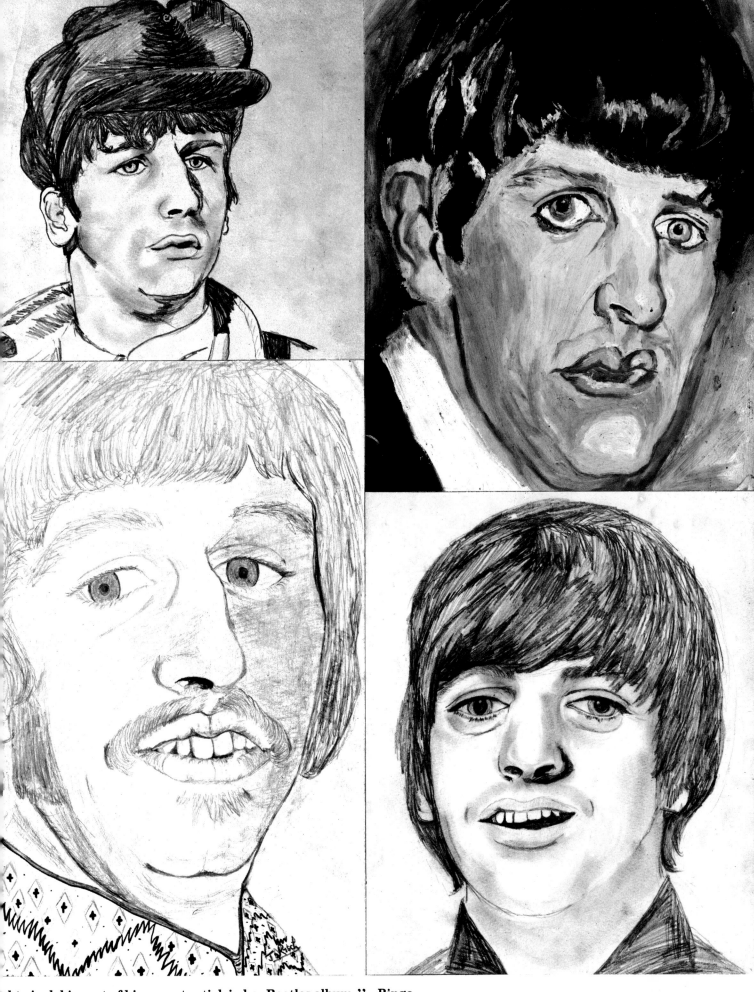

ght pinch him out of his pram to stick in her Beatles album.'' – Ringo

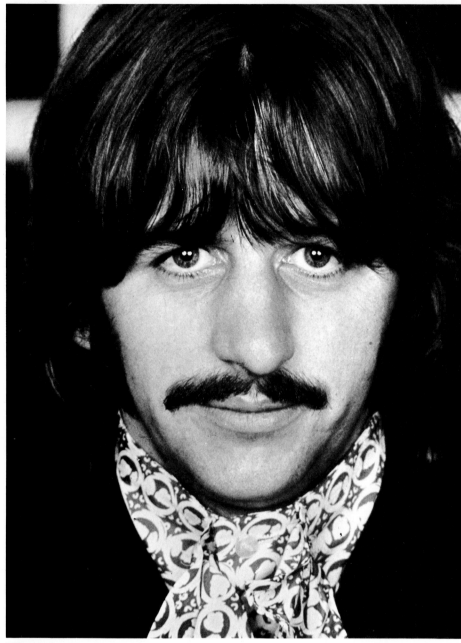

What goes on

What goes on in your heart,
what goes on in your mind?
You are tearing me apart,
when you treat me so unkind,
what goes on in your mind?
The other day I saw you,
as I walked along the road,
but when I saw him with you
I could feel my future fold.
It's so easy for a girl like you to lie,
tell me why?
What goes on in your heart
what goes on in your mind?
You are tearing me apart,
when you treat me so unkind,
what goes on in your mind?
I met you in the morning,
waiting for the tides of time,
but now the tide is turning,
I can see that I was blind.
It's so easy for a girl like you to lie,
tell me why?
What goes on in your heart.
I used to think of no-one else,
but you were just the same,
you didn't even think of me
as someone with a name,
did you mean to break my heart and
watch me die,
tell me why?
What goes on in your heart,
what goes on in your mind?
You are tearing me apart,
when you treat me so unkind,
what goes on in your mind?

"I used to wish that I could write
songs like the others – and I've tried,
but I just can't. I can get the words all
right, but whenever I think of a tune
and sing it to the others they always
say 'Yeah, it sounds like such-a-
thing,' and when they point it out I see
what they mean. But I did get a part
credit as a composer on one – it was
called What Goes On." – Ringo (his
first self-composition was Don't
Pass Me By on The Beatles album –
1968)

Misery

The world is treating me bad, misery.
I'm the kind of guy who never used to cry,
The world is treating me bad, misery.
I've lost her now for sure,
I won't see her no more,
It's gonna be a drag, misery.
I'll remember all the little things we've
done,
Can't she see she'll be the only one,
lonely one,
Send her back to me 'cos ev'ry one can
see,
Without her I will be in misery.
I'll remember all the little things we've
done,
She'll remember and she'll be the only
one, lonely one,
Send her back to me 'cos ev'ry one can
see,
Without her I will be in misery.
Oo in misery. Oo in misery.

37

"Do you remember when everyone began analysing Beatle songs – I don't think I ever understood what some of them

ere supposed to be about." – Ringo

Strawberry Fields forever

Let me take you down,
'cos I'm going to Strawberry Fields.
Nothing is real
and nothing to get hungabout.
Strawberry Fields forever.
Living is easy with eyes closed
Misunderstanding all you see.
It's getting hard to be someone.
But it all works out,
it doesn't matter much to me.
Let me take you down,
'cos I'm going to Strawberry Fields.
Nothing is real
and nothing to get hungabout.
Strawberry Fields forever.
No one I think is in my tree,
I mean it must be high or low.

That is you can't you know tune in.
But it's all right.
That is I think it's not too bad.
Let me take you down,
'cos I'm going to Strawberry Fields.
Nothing is real
and nothing to get hungabout.
Strawberry Fields forever.
Always, no sometimes, think it's me,
but you know I know when it's a dream.
I think I know I mean a 'Yes'.
But it's all wrong.
that is I think I disagree.
Let me take you down,
'cos I'm going to Strawberry Fields.
Nothing is real
and nothing to get hungabout.
Strawberry Fields forever.
Strawberry Fields forever.

39

"Everybody thinks Paul wrote it, but John wrote it for me. He's got a lot of soul has John, you know." -- Ringo

Good night

Now it's time to say good night
Good night sleep tight.
Now the sun turns out his light
Good night sleep tight.
Dream sweet dreams for me
Dream sweet dreams for you.
Close your eyes and I'll close mine
Good night sleep tight.
Now the moon begins to shine
Good night sleep tight.
Dream sweet dreams for me
Dream sweet dreams for you.
Close your eyes and I'll close mine
Good night sleep tight.
Now the sun turns out his light
Good night sleep tight.
Dream sweet dreams for me.
Dream sweet dreams for you.
Good night good night everybody
Everybody everywhere.
Good night.

41

MERSEYSIDE'S OWN ENTERT

MERSE
BEAT

Vol. 1 No. 13   JANUARY 4-18, 1962

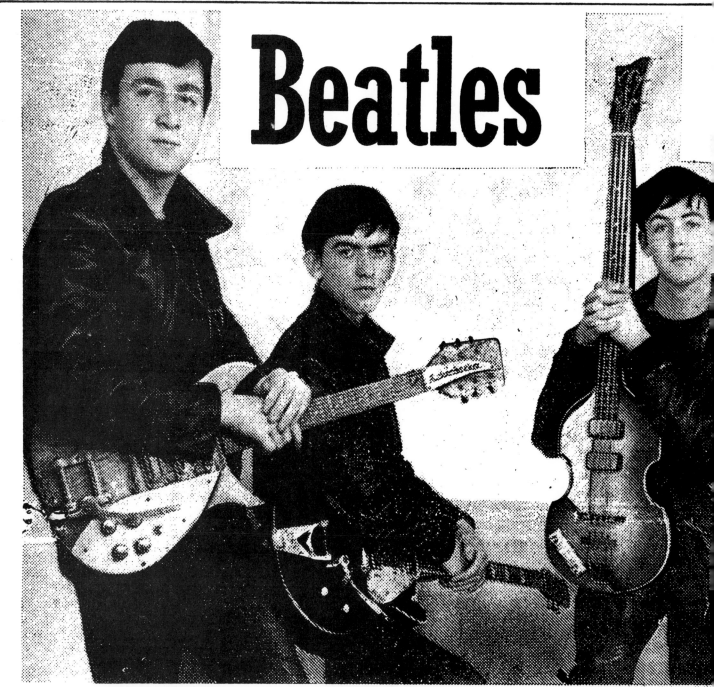

Beatles

JOHN LENNON   GEORGE HARRISON   PAUL McARTRE

NMENTS PAPER

Price THREEPENCE

'op Poll!

FULL RESULTS INSIDE

Cover photograph by Albert Marrion

PETE BEST

''These boys won't make it. Four-
groups are out. Go back to Liverpool
Mr. Epstein – you have a good
business there'' – a major executive of
a major British record company 1962

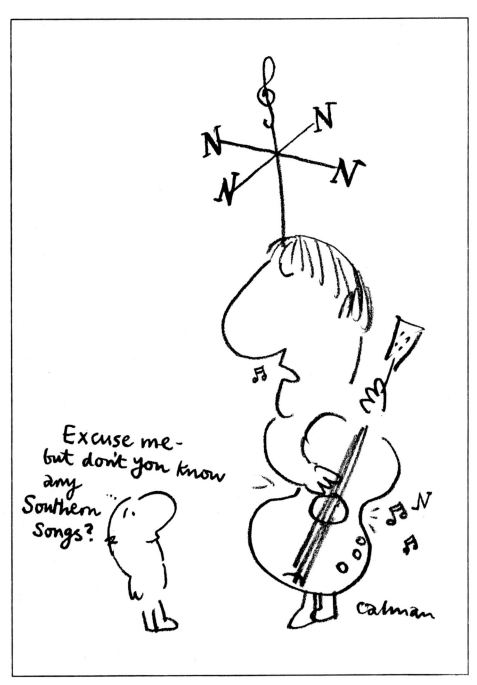

"There's no way to pour £4,000,000 into India and make it right" – Paul

Only a Northern Song

If you're listening to this song
You may think the chords are going wrong
But they're not;
He just wrote it like that.
It doesn't really matter what cords I play
What words I say or time of day it is
As it's only a Northern song
It doesn't really matter what clothes I
wear
Or how I fare or if my hair is brown
When it's only a Northern song.
When you're listening late at night
You may think the band are not quite
right
But they are, they just play it like that
It doesn't really matter what chords I play
What words I say or time of day it is
As it's only a Northern song.
It doesn't really matter what clothes I
wear
Or how I fare or if my hair is brown
When it's only a Northern song.
If you think the harmony
Is a little dark and out of key
You're correct, there's nobody there.
It doesn't really matter what chords I play
What words I say or time of day it is
And I told you there's no one there.

Blackbird

Blackbird singing in the dead of night
Take these broken wings and learn to fly.
All your life
You were only waiting for this moment
to arise.
Blackbird singing in the dead of night
Take these sunken eyes and learn to see.
All your life
You were only waiting for this moment to
be free.
Blackbird fly, Blackbird fly
Into the light of the dark black night.
Blackbird fly, Blackbird fly
Into the light of the dark black night.
Blackbird singing in the dead of night
Take these broken wings and learn to fly.
All your life
You were only waiting for this moment to
arise
You were only waiting for this moment to
arise
You were only waiting for this moment to
arise.

I will

Who knows how long I've loved you.
You know I love you still.
Will I wait a lonely lifetime
If you want me to – I will.
For if I ever saw you
I didn't catch your name.
But it never really mattered
I will always feel the same.
Love you forever and forever.
Love you with all my heart.
Love you whenever we're together.
Love you when we're apart.
And when at last I find you
Your song will fill the air.
Sing it loud so I can hear you.
Make it easy to be near you
For the things you do endear you to me
You know I will.
I will.

I will "I realised that I had been
aware of her for some time. We've
been talking for a long time about
getting married. Then last week
instead of talking about it we
decided to do it. Linda made it
sooner rather than later." – Paul

Here there and everywhere

To lead a better life, I need my love to be
here.
Here, making each day of the year,
changing my life with a wave of her hand.
Nobody can deny that there's something
there.
There, running my hands through her
hair,
both of us thinking how good it can be.
Someone is speaking but she doesn't
know he's there.
I want her ev'rywhere, and if she's beside
me I know I need never care,
but to love her is to meet her ev'rywhere,
knowing that love is to share,
each one believing that love never dies,
watching her eyes and hoping I'm always
there.
I want her ev'rywhere, and if she's beside
me I know I need never care,
but to love her is to meet her ev'rywhere,
knowing that love is to share,
each one believing that love never dies,
watching her eyes and hoping I'm always
there.
To be there and ev'rywhere,
here, there and ev'rywhere.

Back in the U.S.S.R.

Flew in from Miami Beach BOAC.
Didn't get to bed last night.
On the way the paper bag was on my
knee.
Man I had a dreadful flight.
I'm back in the U.S.S.R.
You don't know how lucky you are boy
Back in the U.S.S.R.
Been away so long I hardly knew the
place.
Gee it's good to be back home.
Leave it till tomorrow to unpack my case.
Honey disconnect the phone.
I'm back in the U.S.S.R.
You don't know how lucky you are boy
Back in the U.S. Back in the U.S. Back in
the U.S.S.R.
Well the Ukraine girls really knock me
out.
They leave the West behind.
And Moscow girls make me sing and
shout
That Georgia's always on my mind.
I'm back in the U.S.S.R.
You don't know how lucky you are boys
Back in the U.S.S.R.
Show me round your snow peaked
mountains way down south
Take me to your daddy's farm
Let me hear your balalaika's ringing out
Come and keep your comrade warm.
I'm back in the U.S.S.R.
You don't know how lucky you are boys
Back in the U.S.S.R.

Hey Jude

Hey Jude don't make it bad,
take a sad song and make it better,
remember, to let her into your heart,
then you can start to make it better.
Hey Jude don't be afraid,
you were made to go out and get her,
the minute you let her under your skin,
then you begin to make it better.
And anytime you feel the pain,
Hey Jude refrain,
don't carry the world upon your
shoulders.
For well you know that it's a fool,
who plays it cool,
by making his world a little colder.
Hey Jude don't let me down,
you have found her now go and get her,
remember (Hey Jude) to let her into your
heart,
then you can start to make it better.
So let it out and let it in
Hey Jude begin,
you're waiting for someone to perform
with.
And don't you know that it's just you.
Hey Jude, you'll do,
the movement you need is on your
shoulder.
Hey Jude, don't make it bad,
take a sad song and make it better,
remember to let her under your skin,
then you'll begin to make it better.

Hey Jude "It was going to be 'Hey Jules', but it changed. I was driving down to Weybridge one day to see Cynthia (Lennon) and Julian and I just started singing 'Hey Jules, don't make it bad' and then I changed it to 'Hey Jude'. You know, the way you do."—Paul
Back in the U.S.S.R. "When we first started, our idols were Elvis and Chuck Berry. Now they're Marks and Spencers."—Paul

Got to get you into my life

I was alone, I took a ride,
I didn't know what I would find there.
Another road where maybe I
could see another kind of mind there.
Ooh then I suddenly see you,
ooh did I tell you I need you
ev'ry single day of my life?
You didn't run, you didn't lie,
you knew I wanted just to hold you,
and had you gone, you knew in time

we'd meet again for I had told you.
Ooh you were meant to be near me,
ooh and I want you to hear me,
say we'll be together ev'ry day.
Got to get you into my life.
What can I do, what can I be?
When I'm with you I want to stay there.
If I'm true I'll never leave,
and if I do I know the way there.
Ooh then I suddenly see you,
ooh did I tell you I need you,

ev'ry single day of my life?
Got to get you into my life.
Got to get you into my life.
I was alone, I took a ride,
I didn't know what I would find there.
Another road where maybe I
could see another kind of mind there,
ooh then I suddenly see you,
ooh did I tell you I need you
ev'ry single day of my life?
What are you doing to my life?

"We were influenced by our Tamla Motown bit on this. You see we're influenced by whatever's going."—John

Good morning, good morning

Nothing to do to save his life call his wife
in nothing to say but what a day how's
your boy been
nothing to do it's up to you
I've got nothing to say but it's O.K.
Good morning, good morning,
good morning . . .
Going to work don't want to go feeling
low down
heading for home you start to roam then
you're in town
everybody knows there's nothing doing
everything is closed it's like a ruin
everyone you see is half asleep.
And you're on your own you're in the
street.
Good morning, good morning . . .
After a while you start to smile now you
feel cool.
Then you decide to take a walk by the old
school.
Nothing had changed it's still the same
I've got nothing to say but it's O.K.
Good morning, good morning,
good morning . . .
People running round it's five o'clock.
Everywhere in town it's getting dark.
Everyone you see is full of life.
It's time for tea and meet the wife.
Somebody needs to know the time, glad
that I'm here.
Watching the skirts you start to flirt now
you're in gear.
Go to a show you hope she goes.
I've got nothing to say but it's O.K.
Good morning, good morning,
good morning . . .

**"I often sit at the piano, working at
songs, with the telly on low in the
background. If I'm a bit low and not
getting much done then the words on
the telly come through. That's when
I heard Good Morning, Good
Morning . . . it was a Corn Flakes
advertisement." – John**

Being For The Benefit of Mr Kite ''John has this old poster that says right at the top, 'Pablo Fanques Fair presents the Hendersons For the Benefit of Mr Kite' and it has all the bits that sound strange: 'The Hendersons' – you couldn't make that up. – Paul

Lady Madonna

Lady Madonna children at your feet
wonder how you manage to make ends
meet.
Who finds the money when you pay the
rent?
Did you think that money was heaven
sent?
Friday night arrives without a suitcase
Sunday morning creep in like a nun
Monday's child has learned to tie his
bootlace.
See how they'll run.
Lady Madonna baby at your breast
wonder how you manage to feed the rest.
See how they'll run.
Lady Madonna lying on the bed
listen to the music playing in your head.
Tuesday afternoon is never ending
Wedn'sday morning papers didn't come
Thursday night your stockings needed
mending.
See how they'll run.
Lady Madonna children at your feet
wonder how you manage to make ends
meet.

Being for the benefit of Mr. Kite!

For the benefit of Mr. Kite
there will be a show tonight on
trampoline.
The Hendersons will all be there
late of Pablo Fanques Fair – what a scene.
Over men and horses hoops and garters
lastly through a hogshead of real fire!
In this way Mr. K. will challenge the
world!
The celebrated Mr. K.
performs his feat on Saturday at
Bishopsgate
the Hendersons will dance and sing
as Mr. Kite flies through the ring don't be
late
Messrs. K. and H. assure the public
their production will be second to none
and of course Henry The Horse dances
the waltz!
The band begins at ten to six
when Mr. K. performs his tricks without
a sound
and Mr. H. will demonstrate
ten somersets he'll undertake on solid
ground.
Having been some days in preparation
a splendid time is guaranteed for all
and tonight Mr. Kite is topping the bill.

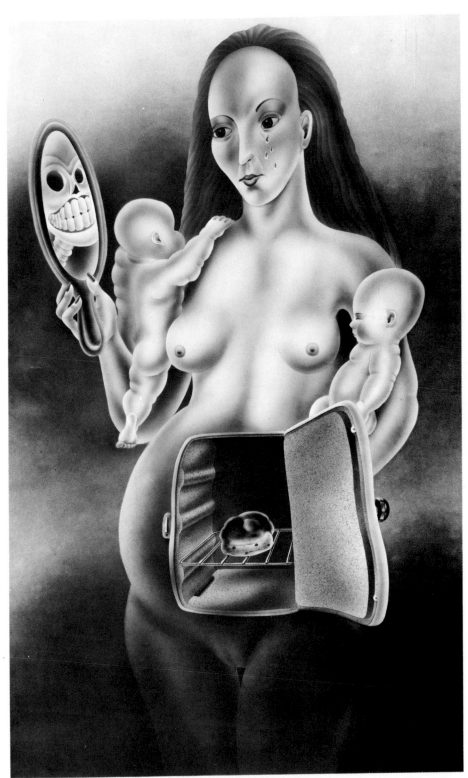

Lady Madonna "It sounds like Elvis doesn't it? No – no it doesn't sound like Elvis. It is Elvis – even those bits where he goes very high." – Ringo

57

"We always got screams up in Scotland, right from the beginning. I suppose they haven't got much else to do up there." – Jo

Genius of the Regency

by William Gaunt

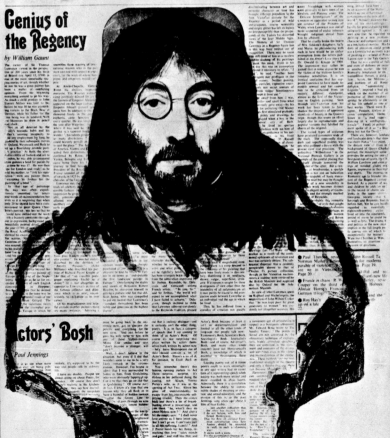

ctors' Bosh

Paul Jennings

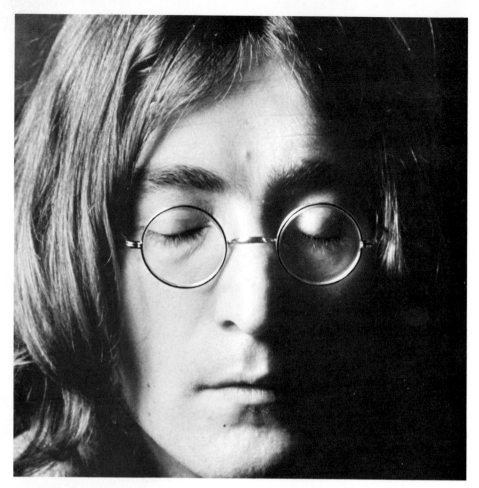

Nowhere man

He's a real Nowhere Man,
sitting in his Nowhere Land,
making all his Nowhere plans for nobody.
Doesn't have a point of view,
knows not where he's going to,
isn't he a bit like you and me?
Nowhere Man please listen,
you don't know what you're missing,
Nowhere Man, the world is at your
command.
He's as blind as he can be,
just sees what he wants to see,
Nowhere Man can you see me at all?
Nowhere Man don't worry,
take your time, don't hurry,
leave it all till somebody else,
lends you a hand.
Doesn't have a point of view,
knows not where he's going to,
isn't he a bit like you and me?
Nowhere Man please listen,
you don't know what you're missing,
Nowhere Man, the world is at your
command.
He's a real Nowhere Man,
sitting in his Nowhere Land,
making all his Nowhere plans for nobody.
Making all his Nowhere plans for nobody.
Making all his Nowhere plans for nobody.

"I was just sitting, trying to think of
a song, and I thought of myself
sitting there, doing nothing and
getting nowhere. Once I'd thought
of that, it was easy. It all came out.
No, I remember now, I'd actually
stopped trying to think of something.
Nothing would come. I was cheesed
off and went for a lie down, having
given up. Then I thought of myself as
Nowhere Man – sitting in his nowhere
land" – John

"At Woolton village fete I met him.
I was a fat schoolboy and, as he
leaned an arm on my shoulder, I
realised that he was drunk. We were
twelve then, but, in spite of his side-
boards, we went on to become teenage
pals." – Paul, in the introduction to
John's first book 'John Lennon In His
Own Write, 1964'

We can work it out

Try to see it my way,
do I have to keep on talking till I can't go
on?
While you see it your way,
run the risk of knowing that our love may
soon be gone.
We can work it out. We can work it out.
Think of what you're saying,
you can get it wrong and still you think
that it's alright,
think of what I'm saying,
we can work it out and get it straight, or
say good-night.
We can work it out. We can work it out.
Life is very short, and there's no time,
for fussing and fighting, my friend,
I have always thought that it's a crime,
so I will ask you once again.
Try to see it my way,
only time will tell if I am right or I am
wrong,
while you see it your way,
there's a chance that we may fall apart
before too long.
Life is very short, and there's no time,
for fussing and fighting, my friend,
I have always thought that it's a crime,
so I will ask you once again.
Try to see it my way,
only time will tell if I am right or I am
wrong,
while you see it your way,
there's a chance that we may fall apart
before too long.
We can work it out. We can work it out.

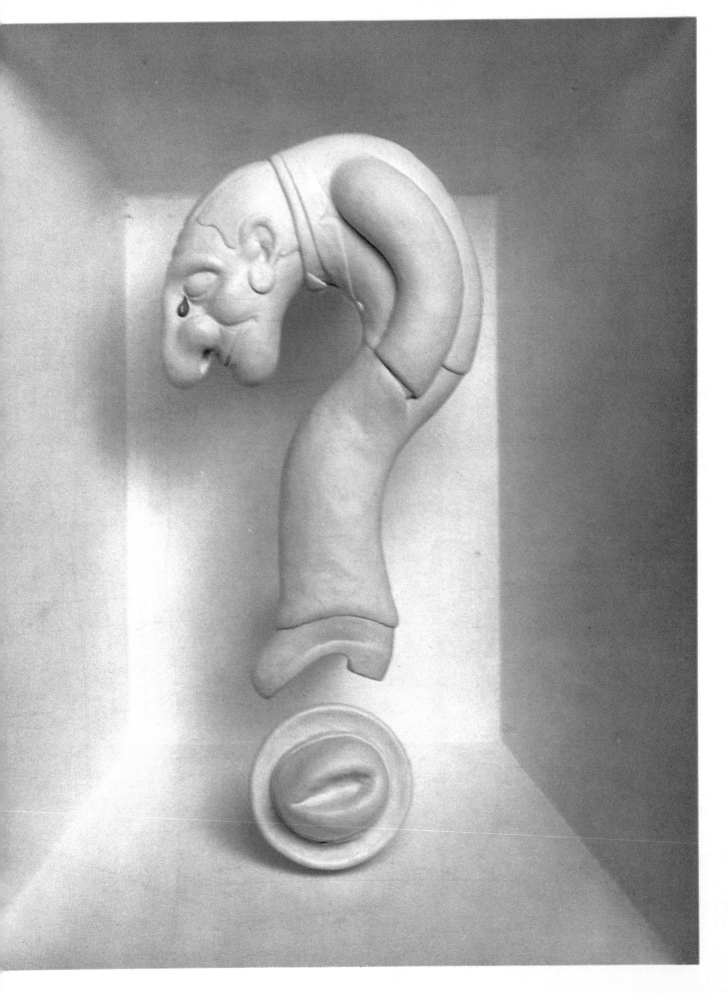

She loves you

She loves you yeh, yeh, yeh,
She loves you yeh, yeh, yeh.
You think you've lost your love,
Well I saw her yesterday– yi – yay,
It's you she's thinking of,
And she told me what to say – yi – yay.
She says she loves you,
And you know that can't be bad,
Yes, she loves you,
And you know you should be glad.
She said you hurt her so,
She almost lost her mind,
And now she says she knows,
You're not the hurting kind.
She says she loves you,
And you know that can't be bad,
Yes, she loves you,
And you know you should be glad.
She loves you yeh, yeh, yeh,
She loves you yeh, yeh, yeh,
And with a love like that,
You know you should be glad.
You know it's up to you,
I think it's only fair,
Pride can hurt you too,
Apologise to her.
Because she loves you,
And you know that can't be bad,
Yes, she loves you,
And you know you should be glad.
She loves you yeh, yeh, yeh,
She loves you yeh, yeh, yeh.
With a love like that,
You know you should be glad.
With a love like that,
You know you should be glad.
With a love like that,
You know you should be glad.
Yeh, yeh, yeh,
Yeh, yeh, yeh.

**''I feel that I'm getting younger.
Even physically. It is partly the diet
because, you see, you are what you
eat. And it is also the fact that I
have met John.'' – Yoko**

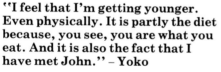

Cry baby cry

Cry baby cry.
Make your mother sigh.
She's old enough to know better.
The king of Marigold was in the kitchen
Cooking breakfast for the queen.
The queen was in the parlour
Playing piano for the children of the king.
Cry baby cry.
Make your mother sigh.
She's old enough to know better.
So cry baby cry.
The king was in the garden
Picking flowers for a friend who came to
play.
The queen was in the playroom
Painting pictures for the children's
holiday.
Cry baby cry.
Make your mother sigh.
She's old enough to know better.
So cry baby cry.
The duchess of Kirkcaldy always smiling
And arriving late for tea.
The duke was having problems
With a message at the local bird and bee.
Cry baby cry.
Make your mother sigh.
She's old enough to know better.
So cry baby cry.
At twelve o'clock a meeting round the
table
For a seance in the dark.
With voices out of nowhere
Put on specially by the children for a lark.
Cry baby cry.
Make your mother sigh.
She's old enough to know better.
So cry baby cry cry cry cry baby.
Make your mother sigh.
She's old enough to know better.
Cry baby cry
cry cry cry
Make your mother sigh.
She's old enough to know better.
So cry baby cry.

**"It's all over now. It's the end, in a
way, isn't it?" – Diane Robbins,
aged 15, of London on the day Paul
was married**

Ticket to ride

I think I'm gonna be sad,
I think it's today yeh,
The girl that's driving me mad,
Is going away.
She's got a ticket to ride,
She's got a ticket to ri – hi – hide,
She's got a ticket to ride,
But she don't care.
She said that living with me,
Is bringing her down yeh,
For she would never be free,
When I was around,
She's got a ticket to ride
She's got a ticket to ri – hi – hide.
She's got a ticket ro ride,
But she don't care.
I don't know why she's riding so high,
She ought to think twice,
She ought to do right by me,
Before she gets to saying goodbye,
She ought to think twice,
She ought to do right by me.

I think I'm gonna be sad,
I think it's today yeh,
The girl that's driving me mad,
Is going away.
She's got a ticket to ride,
She's got a ticket to ri – hi – hide,
She's got a ticket to ride,
But she don't care.
I don't know why she's riding so high,
She ought to think twice,
She ought to do right by me,
Before she gets to saying goodbye,
She ought to think twice,
She ought to do right by me.
She said that living with me,
Is bringing her down yeh,
For she would never be free,
When I was around,
She's got a ticket to ride,
She's got a ticket to ri – hi – hide,
She's got a ticket to ride,
But she don't care.
My baby don't care,
my baby don't care.

Lucy in the sky with diamonds "This one is amazing. People came up and said cunningly 'Right, I get it, LSD' and it was w

at school and brought it home, and he has a schoolmate called Lucy, and John said 'What's that?' and he said 'Lucy in the

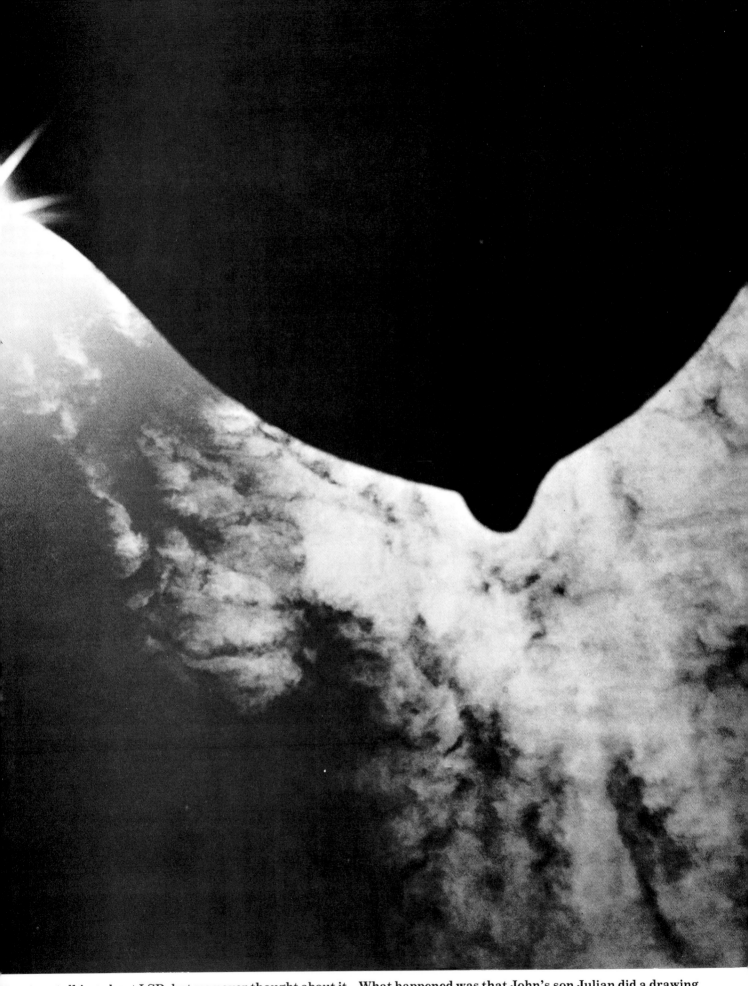

ers were talking about LSD, but we never thought about it.   What happened was that John's son Julian did a drawing h diamonds.'' – Paul

Why don't we do it in the road?

Why don't we do it in the road?
No one will be watching us.
Why don't we do it in the road?

Taxman

Let me tell you how it will be,
There's one for you, nineteen for me,
'Cos I'm the Taxman,
Yeah, I'm the Taxman.
Should five per cent appear too small,
Be thankful I don't take it all,
'Cos I'm the Taxman,
Yeah, I'm the Taxman.
If you drive a car, I'll tax the street,
If you try to sit, I'll tax your seat,
If you get too cold, I'll tax the heat,
If you take a walk, I'll tax your feet.
Taxman.
'Cos I'm the Taxman,
Yeah, I'm the Taxman.
Don't ask me what I want it for
(Taxman Mister Wilson)
If you don't want to pay some more
(Taxman Mister Heath),
'Cos I'm the Taxman,
Yeah, I'm the Taxman.
Now my advice for those who die,
Declare the pennies on your eyes,
'Cos I'm the Taxman,
Yeah, I'm the Taxman.
And you're working for no-one but me,
Taxman.

Lucy in the sky with diamonds

Picture yourself in a boat on a river,
with tangerine trees and marmalade skies
Somebody calls you, you answer quite slowly,
a girl with kaleidoscope eyes.
Cellophane flowers of yellow and green,
towering over your head.
Look for the girl with the sun in her eyes,
and she's gone.
Lucy in the sky with diamonds,
Follow her down to a bridge by a fountain
where rocking horse people eat
marshmallow pies,
everyone smiles as you drift past the flowers,
that grow so incredibly high.
Newspaper taxis appear on the shore,
waiting to take you away.
Climb in the back with your head in the clouds,
and you're gone.
Lucy in the sky with diamonds,
Picture yourself on a train in a station,
with plasticine porters with looking glass ties,
suddenly someone is there at the turnstile,
the girl with kaleidoscope eyes.
Lucy in the sky with diamonds.

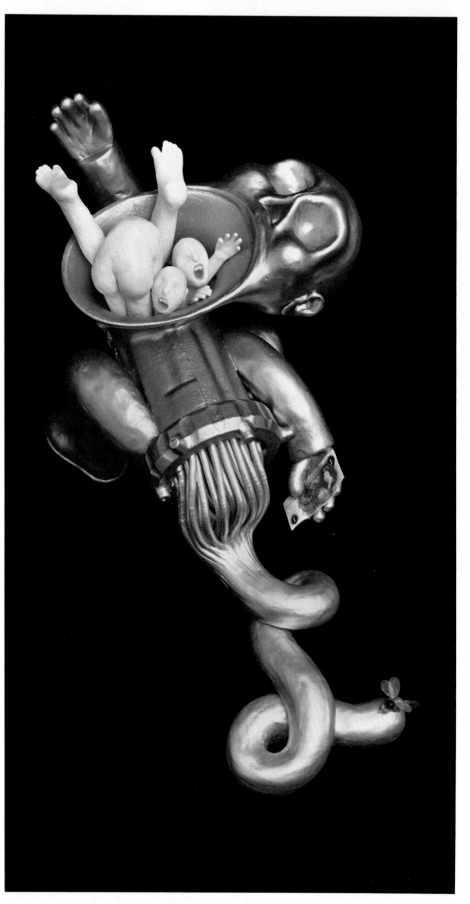

__Taxman__ "I'm down to my last £50,000" – John

Magical Mystery Tour

Roll up – Roll up for the Mystery Tour.
Roll up, roll up for the Mystery Tour.
(roll up) and that's an invitation
Roll up for the Mystery Tour
(roll up) to make a reservation
Roll up for the Mystery Tour
the Magical Mystery Tour is waiting to
take you away
waiting to take you away.
Roll up, roll up for the Mystery Tour
Roll up, roll up for the Mystery Tour
(roll up) we've got ev'rything you need
(roll up) for the Mystery Tour
(roll up) satisfaction guaranteed
Roll up for the Mystery Tour
the Magical Mystery Tour is hoping to
take you away
hoping to take you away now
The Magical Mystery Tour
roll up, roll up for the Mystery Tour.
(roll up) and that's an invitation
Roll up for the Mystery Tour
(roll up) to make a reservation
Roll up for the Mystery Tour
the Magical Mystery Tour is coming to
take you away
coming to take you away
the Magical Mystery Tour is dying to take
you away
dying to take you away – take you today.

**"I suppose if you look at it from the
point of view of good Boxing Day
entertainment we goofed really. My
dad brought the bad news in to me this
morning like the figure of doom.
Perhaps the newspapers are right –
perhaps we're right." – Paul, after
almost universal criticism of their
Magical Mystery Tour television film.**

70

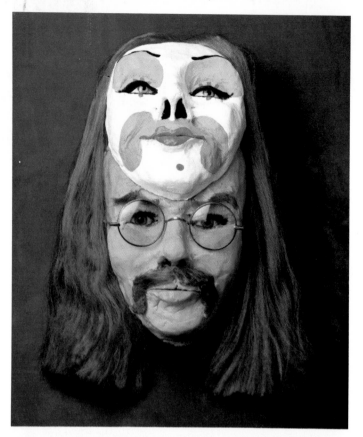

I'm a loser

I'm a loser, I'm a loser,
And I'm not what I appear to be.
Of all the love I have won or have lost,
There is one love I should never have crossed.
She was a girl in a million my friend,
I should have known she would win in the end.
I'm a loser, and I lost someone who's near to me,
I'm a loser, and I'm not what I appear to be.
Although I laugh and I act like a clown,
Beneath this mask, I am wearing a frown,
My tears are falling like rain from the sky,
Is it for her or myself that I cry.
I'm a loser, and I lost someone who's near to me,
I'm a loser, and I'm not what I appear to be.
What have I done to deserve such a fate,
I realise I have left it too late.
And so it's true pride comes before a fall,
I'm telling you so that you won't lose all.
I'm a loser, and I lost someone who's near to me,
I'm a loser and I'm not what I appear to be.

Fixing a hole

I'm fixing a hole where the rain gets in
and stops my mind from wandering
where it will go.
I'm filling the cracks that ran through the door
and kept my mind from wandering
where it will go.
And it really doesn't matter if I'm wrong I'm right
where I belong I'm right
where I belong.
See the people standing there who disagree and never win
and wonder why they don't get in my door.
I'm painting the room in a colourful way
and when my mind is wandering
there I will go.
And it really doesn't matter if
I'm wrong I'm right
where I belong I'm right
where I belong.
Silly people run around they worry me
and never ask me why they don't get past my door.
I'm taking the time for a number of things
that weren't important yesterday
and I still go.
I'm fixing a hole where the rain gets in
and stops my mind from wandering
where it will go.

Rocky Raccoon

Now somewhere in the black mountain
hills of Dakota
There lived a young boy named Rocky
Raccoon.
And one day his woman ran off with
another guy.
Hit young Rocky in the eye Rocky didn't
like that.
He said I'm gonna get that boy.
So one day he walked into town
Booked himself a room in the local saloon.
Rocky Raccoon checked into his room
Only to find Gideon's Bible.
Rocky had come equipped with a gun
To shoot off the legs of his rival.
His rival it seems had broken his dreams
By stealing the girl of his fancy.
Her name was Magill and she called
herself Lill
But everyone knew her as Nancy.
Now she and her man who called
himself Dan
Were in the next room at the hoe down.
Rocky burst in and grinning a grin.
He said Danny boy this is a showdown
But Daniel was hot – he drew first and
shot
And Rocky collapsed in the corner.
Now the doctor came in stinking of gin
And proceeded to lie on the table.
He said Rocky you met your match.
And Rocky said, Doc it's only a scratch
And I'll be better, I'll be better doc as
soon as I am able.
Now Rocky Raccoon he fell back in his
room
Only to find Gideon's Bible.
Gideon checked out and he left it no
doubt
To help with good Rocky's revival.

Norwegian wood

I once had a girl,
or I should say
she once had me.
She showed me her room,
isn't it good?
Norwegian wood.
She asked me to stay and she told me to
sit anywhere,
so I looked around and I noticed there
wasn't a chair.
I sat on a rug
biding my time,
drinking her wine.
We talked until two,
and then she said,
''It's time for bed''.
She told me she worked in the morning
and started to laugh,
I told her I didn't, and crawled off to
sleep in the bath.
And when I awoke
I was alone,
this bird had flown,
so I lit a fire,
isn't it good?
Norwegian wood.

Help

Help! I need somebody,
help! Not just anybody,
help! You know I need someone,
help!
When I was younger, so much younger
than today,
I never needed anybody's help in any
way,
but now these days are gone I'm not so
self assured,
now I find I've changed my mind I've
opened up the doors.
Help me if you can, I'm feeling down,
and I do appreciate you being around,
help me get my feet back on the ground,
won't you please please help me?
And now my life has changed in oh so
many ways,
my independence seems to vanish in the
haze,
but ev'ry now and then I feel so insecure,
I know that I just need you like I've
never done before.
Help me if you can, I'm feeling down,
and I do appreciate you being round,
help me get my feet back on the ground,
won't you please please help me?
When I was younger, so much younger
than today,
I never needed anybody's help in any
way,
but now these days are gone I'm not so
self assured,
now I find I've changed my mind I've
opened up the doors.
Help me if you can I'm feeling down,
and I do appreciate you being round,
help me get my feet back on the ground,
won't you please please help me? Help
me. Help me.

**'Help' was great fun but it wasn't our
film. We were sort of guest stars.
It was fun, but basically as an idea for
a film it was a bit wrong for us.'' – Paul**

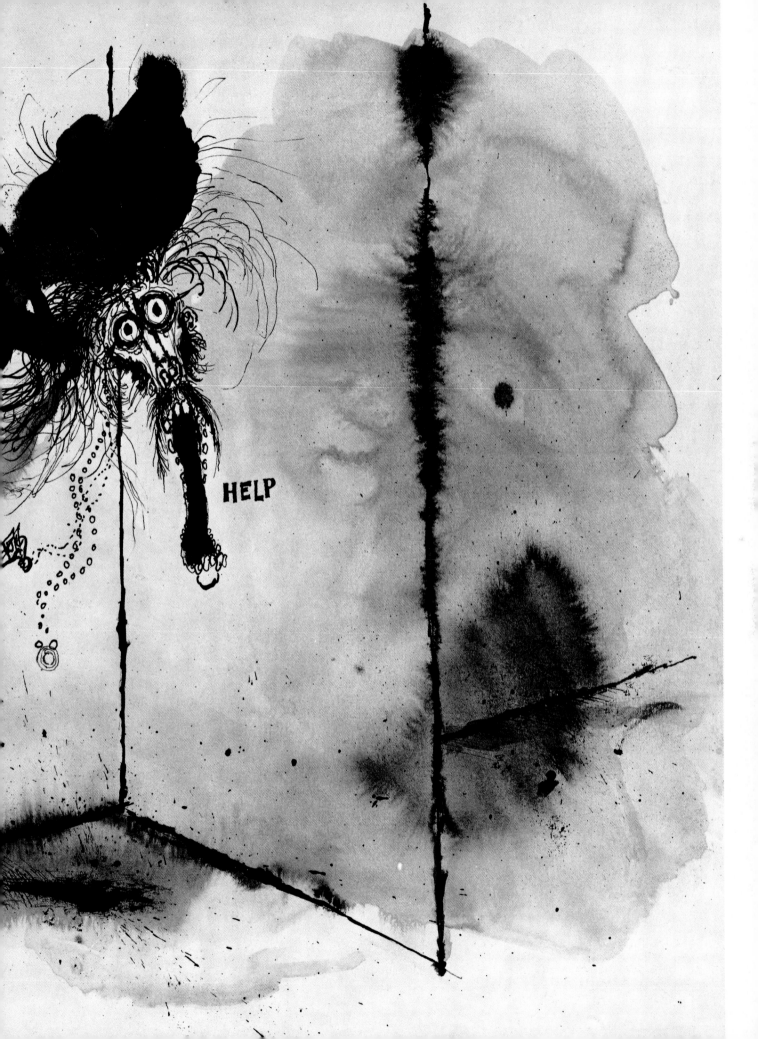

Sexy Sadie

Sexy Sadie what have you done.
You made a fool of everyone.
You made a fool of everyone.
Sexy Sadie ooh what have you done.
Sexy Sadie you broke the rules.
You layed it down for all to see.
You layed it down for all to see.
Sexy Sadie oooh you broke the rules.
One sunny days the world was waiting
for a lover.
She came along to turn on everyone.
Sexy Sadie the greatest of them all.
Sexy Sadie how did you know.
The world was waiting just for you.
The world was waiting just for you.
Sexy Sadie oooh how did you know.
Sexy Sadie you'll get yours yet.
However big you think you are.
However big you think you are.
Sexy Sadie oooh you'll get yours yet.
We gave her everything we owned just to
sit at her table
Just a smile would lighten everything
Sexy Sadie she's the latest and the
greatest of them all.
She made a fool of everyone
Sexy Sadie.
However big you think you are
Sexy Sadie.

''You'll get yours yet'' – John

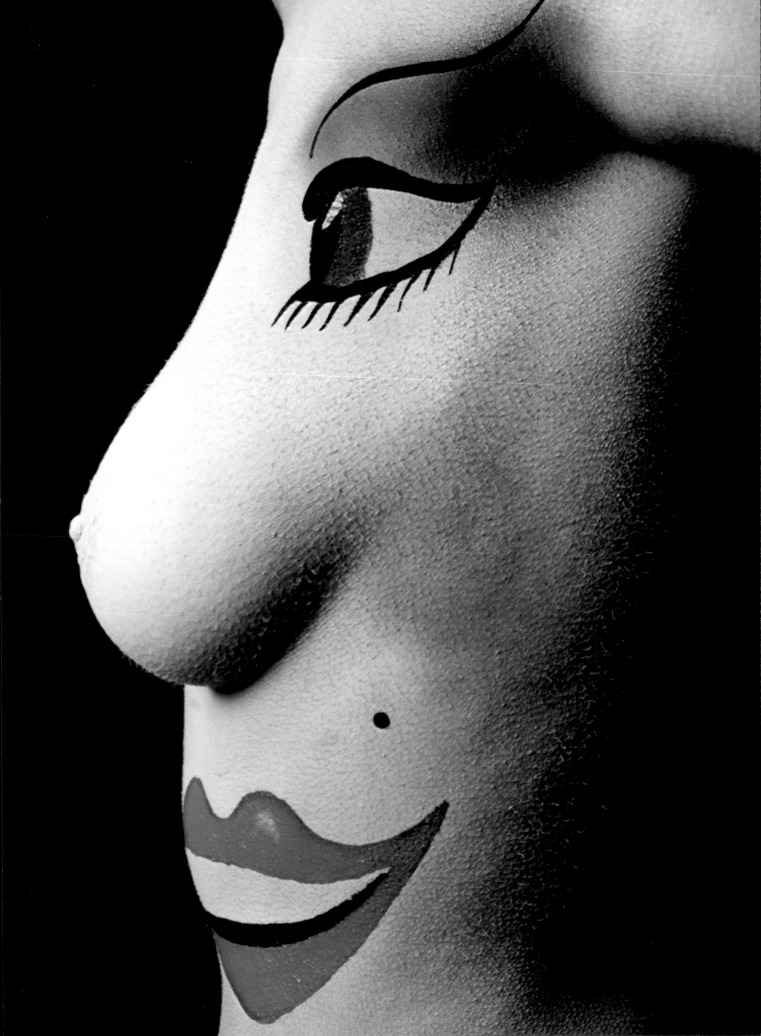

I am the walrus

I am he as you are he as you are me and
we are all together.
See how they run like pigs from a gun
see how they fly,
I'm crying.
Sitting on a cornflake – waiting for the
van to come.
Corporation teashirt, stupid bloody
Tuesday man you been a naughty boy you
let your face grow long.
I am the eggman oh, they are the eggmen –
Oh I am the walrus GOO GOO G'JOOB.
Mr. City policeman sitting pretty little
policeman in a row,
see how they fly like Lucy in the sky –
see how they run
I'm crying – I'm crying I'm crying.
Yellow matter custard dripping from a
dead dog's eye.
Crabalocker fishwife pornographic
priestess boy you been a naughty girl,
you let your knickers down.

I am the eggman oh, they are the eggmen –
Oh I am the walrus. GOO GOO G'JOOB.
Sitting in an English garden waiting for
the sun,
If the sun don't come, you get a tan from
standing in the English rain.
I am the eggman oh, they are the eggmen –
Oh I am the walrus. G'JOOB, G'GOO,
G'JOOB.
Expert texpert choking smokers don't you
think the joker laughs at you?
Ha ha ha!
See how they smile, like pigs in a sty, see
how they snied.
I'm crying.
Semolina pilchards climbing up the Eiffel
Tower.
Elementary penguin singing Hare
Krishna man you should have seen them
kicking Edgar Allen Poe.
I am the eggman oh, they are the eggmen –
Oh I am the walrus GOO GOO GOO JOOB
GOO GOO GOO JOOB GOO GOO
GOOOOOOOOOOOJOOOOOB.

Nobody I know

Nobody I know could love me more than
you,
You can give me so much love it seems
untrue,
Listen to the bird who sings it to the tree,
And then when you've heard him see if
you agree,
Nobody I know could love you more than
me.
Ev'rywhere I go the sun comes shining
through,
Ev'ryone I know is sure it shines for you,
Even in my dreams I look into your eyes,
Suddenly it seems I've found a paradise,
Ev'rywhere I go the sun comes shining
through.
It means so much to be a part of a heart of

a wonderful one,
When other lovers are gone we'll live on,
We'll live on.
Even in my dreams I look into your eyes,
Suddenly it seems I've found a paradise,
Ev'rywhere I go the sun comes shining
through.
Nobody I know could love me more than
you,
You can give me so much love it seems
untrue,
Listen to the bird who sings it to the tree,
And then when you've heard him see if
you agree,
Nobody I know could love you more than
me.
Nobody I know could love you more than
me.

I am the walrus "All these financial takeovers and things – it's just like Monopoly – **John**

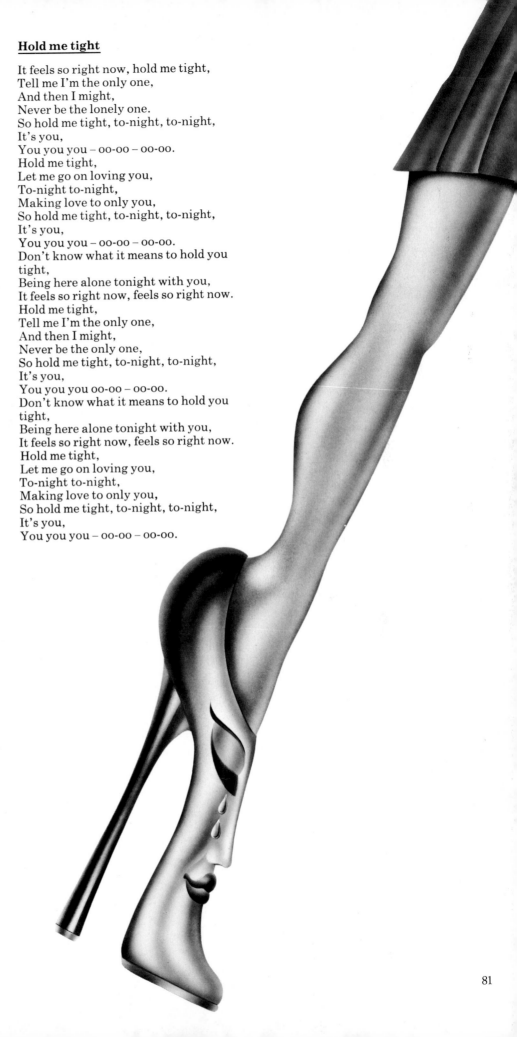

She's leaving home

Wednesday morning at five o'clock as the day begins
silently closing her bedroom door
leaving the note that she hoped would say more
she goes downstairs to the kitchen
clutching her handkerchief
quietly turning the backdoor key
stepping outside she is free.
She (We gave her most of our lives)
is leaving (Sacrificed most of our lives)
home (We gave her everything money could buy)
she's leaving home after living alone
for so many years. Bye, bye.
Father snores as his wife gets into her dressing gown
picks up the letter that's lying there
standing alone at the top of the stairs
she breaks down and cries to her husband
daddy our baby's gone.
Why should she treat us so thoughtlessly
how could she do this to me.
She (We never thought of ourselves)
is leaving (Never a thought for ourselves)
home (We struggled hard all our lives to get by)
she's leaving home after living alone
for so many years. Bye, bye.
Friday morning at nine o'clock she is far away
waiting to keep the appointment she made
meeting a man from the motor trade.
She (What did we do that was wrong)
is leaving (We didn't know it was wrong)
home (Fun is the one thing that money can't buy)
something inside that was always denied
for so many years. Bye, bye.
She's leaving home bye bye.

"There was a Daily Mirror story about this girl who left home and her father said: 'We gave her everything, I don't know why she left home.' But he didn't give her that much, not what she wanted when she left home." – Paul

Hold me tight

It feels so right now, hold me tight,
Tell me I'm the only one,
And then I might,
Never be the lonely one.
So hold me tight, to-night, to-night,
It's you,
You you you – oo-oo – oo-oo.
Hold me tight,
Let me go on loving you,
To-night to-night,
Making love to only you,
So hold me tight, to-night, to-night,
It's you,
You you you – oo-oo – oo-oo.
Don't know what it means to hold you tight,
Being here alone tonight with you,
It feels so right now, feels so right now.
Hold me tight,
Tell me I'm the only one,
And then I might,
Never be the only one,
So hold me tight, to-night, to-night,
It's you,
You you you oo-oo – oo-oo.
Don't know what it means to hold you tight,
Being here alone tonight with you,
It feels so right now, feels so right now.
Hold me tight,
Let me go on loving you,
To-night to-night,
Making love to only you,
So hold me tight, to-night, to-night,
It's you,
You you you – oo-oo – oo-oo.

Don't let me down ''I never signed a contract with the Beatles. I had given my word about what I intended to do, and t

enough. I abided by the terms and no-one ever worried about me not signing it.''—Brian Epstein

Don't let me down

Don't let me down
Don't let me down
Don't let me down
Don't let me down
Nobody ever loved me like she does
Ooh she does. Yes she does
And if somebody loved me
Like she do to me
Ooh she do me. Yes she does
Don't let me down
Don't let me down
Don't let me down
Don't let me down
I'm in love for the first time
Don't you know it's going to last
It's a love that lasts forever
It's a love that has no past
Don't let me down
Don't let me down
Don't let me down
Don't let me down
And from the first time that she really
done me
Ooh she done me. She done me good
I guess nobody ever really done me
Ooh she done me
She done me
She done me good
Don't let me down
Don't let me down
Don't let me down
Don't let me down

Doctor Robert

Ring my friend I said you'd call Doctor
Robert,
day or night he'll be there anytime at all,
Doctor Robert,
Doctor Robert, you're a new and better
man,
he helps you to understand,
he does ev'rything he can, Doctor Robert.
If you are down he'll pick you up, Doctor
Robert,
take a drink from his special cup, Doctor
Robert,
Doctor Robert, he's a man you must
believe,
helping ev'ry one in need,
no-one can succeed like Doctor Robert.
Well, well, well, you're feeling fine,
well, well, well, he'll make you, Doctor
Robert.
My friend works with the National
Health, Doctor Robert,
don't pay money just to see yourself with
Doctor Robert,
Doctor Robert, you're a new and better
man,
he helps you to understand,
he does ev'rything he can, Doctor Robert.
Well, well, well, you're feeling fine,
well, well, well, he'll make you Doctor
Robert.
Ring my friend I said you'd call
Doctor Robert.

"Well, he's like a joke. There's some fellow in New York, and in the States
we'd hear people say 'You can get everything off him;
any pills you want . . .' That's what Dr. Roberts is all about, just a pill
doctor who sees you all right." – Paul

The above picture contains clues to thirteen Beatles' song titles, for example, the eagle on John's eye refers to the line 'The eagle picks my eyes, the worm he likcs my bones' from Yer Blues. Can you find the other twelve titles? Answers on page 138.

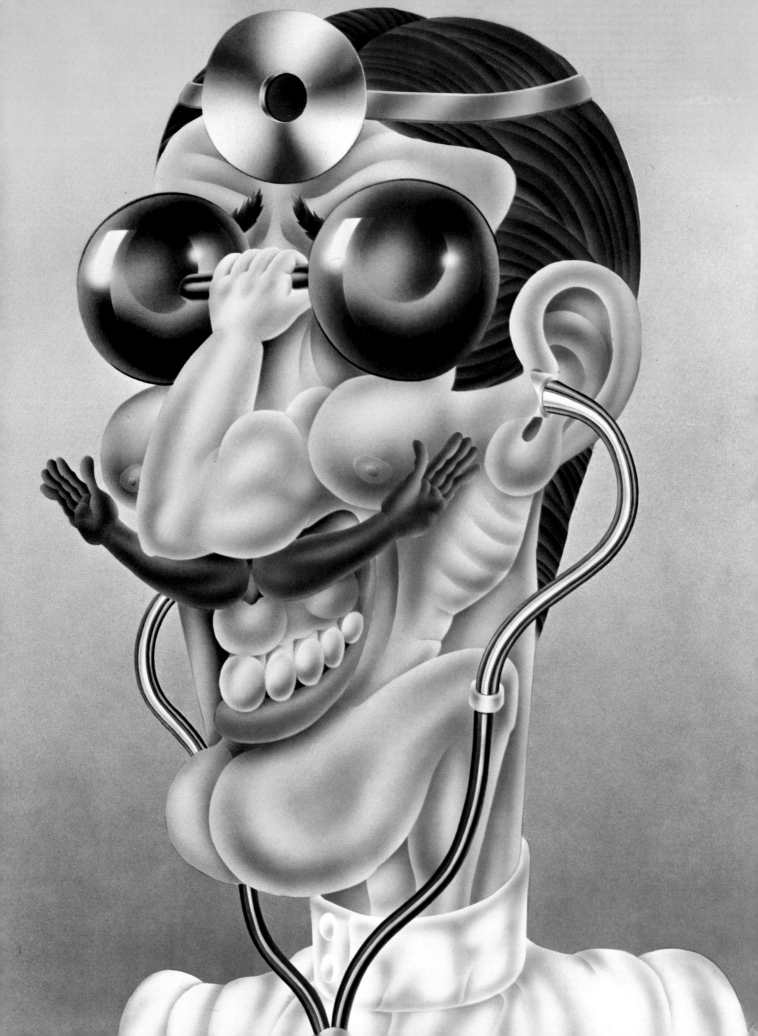

Everybody's got something to hide except for me and my monkey

Come on come on come on come on
Come on is such a joy
Come on is such a joy
Come on take it easy
Come on take it easy.
Take it easy take it easy.
Everybody's got something to hide except
for me and my monkey.
The deeper you go the higher you fly.
The higher you fly the deeper you go.
So come on come on
Come on is such a joy
Come on is such a joy
Come on make it easy
Come on make it easy.
Take it easy take it easy.
Everybody's got something to hide
except for me and my monkey.
Your inside is out and your outside is in.
Your outside is in and your inside is out.
So come on come on
Come on is such a joy
Come on is such a joy
Come on make it easy
Come on make it easy
Make it easy make it easy.
Everybody's got something to hide except
for me and my monkey.

**"I'm very shy, John is shy too." –
Yoko Ono**

Love you to

Each day just goes so fast,
I turn around, it's past,
you don't get time to hand a sign on me.
Love me while you can,
before I'm a dead old man.
A life-time is so short,
a new one can't be bought,
but what you've got means such a lot to me.
Make love all day long,
make love singing songs.
Make love all day long,
make love singing songs.
There's people standing round,
who'll screw you in the ground,
they'll fill you in with all their sins,
you'll see.
I'll make love to you,
if you want me to.

**"I began to write more songs when I
had more time, especially when we
began to stop touring. Having Indian
things so much in my head it was
bound to come out."   George**

"The fans are really what it's all been about. And of course we like them. But there are times when we want to be left to ha

me privacy – when they can be a nuisance. But I suppose it's just part of the job.'' – Paul

I'm only sleeping

When I wake up early in the morning,
Lift my head, I'm still yawning.
When I'm in the middle of a dream,
Stay in bed, float up stream (float up
stream),
Please don't wake me, no, don't shake
me,
Leave me where I am, I'm only sleeping.
Everybody seems to think I'm lazy.
I don't mind, I think they're crazy
Running everywhere at such a speed,
Till they find there's no need (there's no
need),
Please don't spoil my day, I'm miles away,
And after all, I'm only sleeping.
Keeping an eye on the world going by my
window,
Taking my time, lying there and staring
at the ceiling,
Waiting for a sleepy feeling.
Please don't spoil my day, I'm miles
away,
And after all I'm only sleeping.
Keeping an eye on the world going by my
window,
Taking my time.
When I wake up early in the morning,
Lift my head, I'm still yawning,
When I'm in the middle of a dream,
Stay in bed, float up stream (float up
stream),
Please don't wake me, no, don't shake me,
Leave me where I am, I'm only sleeping.

Love me do

Love, love me do,
you know I love you.
I'll always be true
so please love me do, who ho love me do.
Love, love me do,
you know I love you.
I'll always be true
so please love me do, who ho love me do.
Someone to love, somebody new.
Someone to love, someone like you.
Love, love me do,
you know I love you
I'll always be true
so please love me do, who ho love me do.
Love, love me do,
you know I love you.
I'll always be true
so please love me do, who ho love me do.

**"That's what we want to get back to –
simplicity. You can't have anything
simpler, yet more meaningful than
'love, love me – do.' That's just what
it means. I think I slagged off school
to write that one with John when we
first started." – Paul**

Yellow submarine
"I knew it would get connotations, but it really was a children's song. I just loved the idea of kids singing it." – Paul

94

—D

I saw her standing there

Well, she was just seventeen,
You know what I mean,
And the way she looked was way beyond
compare,
So how could I dance with another,
oh when I saw her standing there
Well she looked at me,
and I, I could see,
that before too long I'd fall in love with
her,
she wouldn't dance with another,
oh when I saw her dancing there.
Well my heart went zoom when I crossed
that room,
and I held her hand in mine.
Oh we danced through the night,
and we held each other tight,
and before too long I fell in love with her,
now I'll never dance with another,
oh when I saw her standing there.
Well my heart went zoom when I cross'd
that room,
and I held her hand in mine.
Oh we danced through the night,
and we held each other tight,
and before too long I fell in love with her,
now I'll never dance with another,
oh since I saw her standing there.
Oh since I saw her standing there.

Yellow submarine

In the town where I was born,
lived a man who sailed the sea,
and he told us of his life,
in the land of submarines.
So we sailed on to the sun,
till we found the sea of green,
and we lived beneath the waves,
in our yellow submarine.
We all live in a yellow submarine,
yellow submarine, yellow submarine,
we all live in a yellow submarine,
yellow submarine, yellow submarine.
And our friends are all aboard,
many more of them live next door,
and the band begins to play.
We all live in a yellow submarine,
yellow submarine, yellow submarine,
we all live in a yellow submarine,
yellow submarine, yellow submarine.
As we live a life of ease,
everyone of us has all we need,
sky of blue and sea of green,
in our yellow submarine.
We all live in a yellow submarine,
yellow submarine, yellow submarine,
we all live in a yellow submarine,
yellow submarine, yellow submarine.

"I was just thinking of nice words like Sergeant Pepper and Lonely Hearts Club, and they came together for no reason . . . They're a bit of a brass band in a way, but also a rock band because they've got the San Francisco thing."
Paul

Sgt. Pepper's Lonely Hearts Club Band

It was twenty years ago today, that
Sgt. Pepper taught the band to play
they've been going in and out of style
but they're guaranteed to raise a smile.
So may I introduce to you
the act you've known for all these years,
Sgt. Pepper's Lonely Hearts Club Band.
We're Sgt. Pepper's Lonely Hearts Club
Band,
we hope you will enjoy the show,
We're Sgt. Pepper's Lonely Hearts Club
Band,
sit back and let the evening go.

Sgt. Pepper's lonely, Sgt. Pepper's
lonely,
Sgt. Pepper's Lonely Hearts Club Band.
It's wonderful to be here,
it's certainly a thrill.
You're such a lovely audience,
we'd like to take you home with us,
we'd love to take you home.
I don't really want to stop the show,
but I thought you might like to know,
that the singer's going to sing a song,
and he wants you all to sing along.
So may I introduce to you
the one and only Billy Shears
and Sgt. Pepper's Lonely Hearts Club
Band.

hard day's night

It's been a hard day's night,
And I've been working like a dog,
It's been a hard day's night,
I should be sleeping like a log,
But when I get home to you,
I find the thing that you do,
Will make me feel alright.
You know I work all day,
To get you money to buy you things,
And it's worth it just to hear you say,
You're gonna give me ev'rything,
So why on earth should I moan,
'Cos when I get you alone,
You know I feel okay.
When I'm home ev'rything seems to be
right,
When I'm home feeling you holding me
tight, tight, yeh.
It's been a hard day's night,
And I've been working like a dog,

It's been a hard day's night,
I should be sleeping like a log,
But when I get home to you,
I find the things that you do,
Will make me feel alright.
So why on earth should I moan,
'Cos when I get you alone,
You know I feel okay.
When I'm home ev'rything seems to be
right,
When I'm home feeling you holding me
tight, tight, yeh.
It's been a hard day's night,
And I've been working like a dog,
It's been a hard day's night,
I should be sleeping like a log,
But when I get home to you,
I find the things that you do,
Will make me feel alright.
You know I feel alright.
You know I feel alright.

**"It wasn't so much that Brian
Epstein discovered the Beatles but
that the Beatles discovered Brian
Epstein" – Paul**

Baby, you're a rich man

How does it feel to be
One of the beautiful people?
Now that you know who you are
What do you want to be?
And have you travelled very far?
Far as the eye can see.
How does it feel to be
one of the beautiful people?
How often have you been there?
Often enough to know.
What did you see, when you were there?
Nothing that doesn't show.
Baby you're a rich man,
Baby you're a rich man,
Baby you're a rich man too.
You keep all your money in a big brown
bag
inside a zoo.
What a thing to do.
Baby you're a rich man,
Baby you're a rich man,
Baby you're a rich man too.
How does it feel to be
One of the beautiful people?
Tuned to A natural E
Happy to be that way.
Now that you've found another key
What are you going to play?
Baby you're a rich man,
Baby you're a rich man,
Baby you're a rich man too.
You keep all your money in a big brown
bag
inside a zoo
What a thing to do.
Baby you're a rich man . . .

"I want money just to be rich" – John

Yesterday

Yesterday,
all my troubles seemed so far away,
now it looks as though they're here to
stay,
oh, I believe in yesterday.
Suddenly,
I'm not half the man I used to be,
there's a shadow hanging over me,
oh, yesterday came suddenly.
Why she had to go I don't know,
she wouldn't say,
I said something wrong,
now I long for yesterday.
Yesterday,
love was such an easy game to play,
now I need a place to hide away,
oh, I believe in yesterday.
Why she had to go I don't know,
she wouldn't say,
I said something wrong,
now I long for yesterday.
Yesterday,
love was such an easy game to play,
now I need a place to hide away,
oh, I believe in yesterday.
Mm mm mm mm mm mm mm.

**"I woke up one morning and went to the piano.
And I just, you know, started playing it. And this tune came.
Because that's what happens you know,
they just come. But I couldn't think of any words
for it so originally I called it 'Scrambled Egg'. For a couple of
mornings that was what it was called. Then
I thought of 'Yesterday' and the words started to come
and we had a song." – Paul**

Revolution ''The trouble is that so much of the pop and record business is being run by people who don't have a clue what it is about'' – Paul

103

Revolution

You say you want a revolution
Well, you know
we all want to change the world.
You tell me that it's evolution,
Well, you know
we all want to change the world.
But when you talk about destruction,
Don't you know that you can count me
out.
Don't you know it's going to be alright,
Alright, alright.
You say you got a real solution
Well, you know
we'd all love to see the plan.
You ask me for a contribution,
Well, you know
we're doing what we can.
But if you want money for people with
minds that hate,
All I can tell you is brother you have to
wait.
Don't you know it's going to be alright,
Alright, alright.
You say you'll change a constitution
well, you know
we all want to change your head.
You tell me it's the institution,
well, you know
you better free your mind instead.
But if you go carrying pictures of
Chairman Mao,
You ain't going to make it with anyone
anyhow.
Don't you know it's going to be alright,
alright, alright.

Tell me what you see

If you let me take your heart I will prove
to you,
we will never be apart if I'm part of you,
open up your eyes now tell me what you
see,
it is no surprise now what you see is me.
Big and black the clouds may be time will
pass away,
if you put your trust in me I'll make bright
your day.
Look into these eyes now, tell me what
you see,
don't you realise now what you see is me.
Tell me what you see.
Listen to me one more time how can I get
through,
can't you try to see that I'm trying to get
to you,
open up your eyes now tell me what you
see,
it is no surprise now, what you see is me.
Tell me what you see.
Listen to me one more time how can I get
through.
Listen to me one more time, how can I get
through,
can't you try to see that I'm trying to get
to you,
open up your eyes now tell me what you
see,
it is no surprise what you see is me.

♭ for I don't care too much for money
for money can't buy me love ♯

Can't buy me love

Can't buy me love, love,
Can't buy me love.
I'll buy you a diamond ring my friend,
If it makes you feel alright,
I'll get you anything my friend,
If it makes you feel alright,
For I don't care too much for money,
For money can't buy me love.
I'll give you all I've got to give,
If you say you love me too,
I may not have a lot to give,
But what I've got I'll give to you,
For I don't care too much for money,
For money can't buy me love.
Can't buy me love, ev'rybody tells me so,
Can't buy me love, no, no, no, no.
Say you don't want no diamond ring,
And I'll be satisfied,
Tell me that you want those kind of
things,
That money just can't buy,
For I don't care too much for money,
For money can't buy me love.
Can't buy me love, ev'rybody tells me so,
Can't buy me love, no, no, no, no.
Say you don't want no diamond ring,
And I'll be satisfied,
Tell me that you want those kind of
things,
That money just can't buy
For I don't care too much for money,
For money can't buy me love.
Can't buy me love, ev'rybody tells me so,
Can't buy me love, no, no, no, no.
Can't buy me love, love,
Can't buy me love.

"Personally, I think you can put any
interpretation you want on anything,
but when someone suggests that 'Can't
Buy Me Love' is about a prostitute, I
draw the line. That's going too far." –
Paul

John Glashan

The fool on the hill

Day after day, alone on a hill,
the man with the foolish grin is keeping
perfectly still.
But nobody wants to know him,
they can see that he's just a fool
and he never gives an answer.
But the fool on the hill sees the sun going
down
and the eyes in his head see the world
spinning round.
Well on the way, head in a cloud,
the man of a thousand voices talking
perfectly loud.
But nobody ever hears him
or the sound he appears to make
and he never seems to notice.
But the fool on the hill sees the sun
going down
and the eyes in his head see the world
spinning round.
And nobody seems to like him,
they can tell what he wants to do
and he never shows his feelings.
But the fool on the hill sees the sun going
down
and the eyes in his head see the world
spinning round.
He never listens to them,
he knows that they're the fools.
They don't like him.
The fool on the hill sees the sun going
down
and the eyes in his head see the world
spinning round.

**"We made a mistake, the Maharishi
is human. For a while we thought he
wasn't. We believe in meditation but
not the Maharishi and his scene.
We're finished with that bit of it." –
John**

The Inner Light

Without going out of my door
I can know all things on earth.
Without looking out of my window
I could know the ways of heaven.
The farther one travels,
The less one knows,
The less one knows.
Without going out of your door
You can know all things on earth.
Without looking out of your window
You can know the ways of heaven.
The farther one travels,
The less one knows,
The less one knows.
Arrive without travelling.
See all without looking.
(See all without looking).

**'George wrote this. Forget the
Indian music and listen to the
melody. Don't you think it's a
beautiful melody? It's really lovely.'
– Paul**

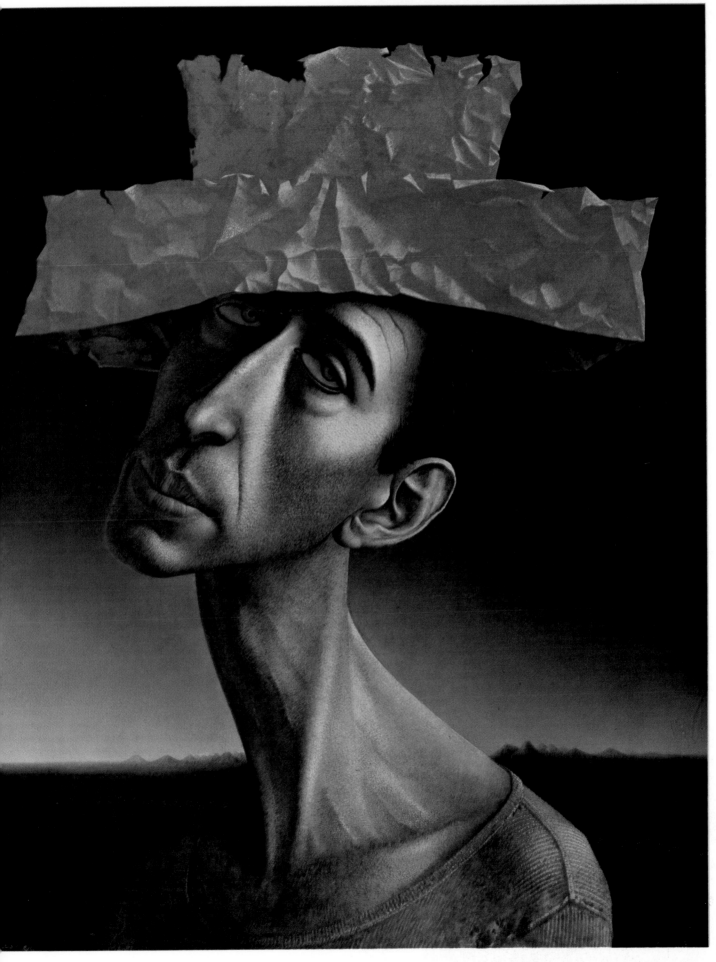

Oh George, and you're such a little man!!.

"Drop me a line with all the news, I've got a little bit behind the Times down here!"

Day tripper

Got a good reason for taking the easy way out,
got a good reason for taking the easy way out – now,
she was a day tripper,
one way ticket, yeh,
it took me so long to find out, and I found out.
She's a big teaser, she took me half the way there,
she's a big teaser, she took me half the way there – now,
she was a day tripper,
one way ticket, yeh,
it took me so long to find out, and I found out.
Tried to please her, she only played one night stands,
tried to please her, she only played one night stands – now,
she was a day tripper,
Sunday driver, yeh,
it took me so long to find out, and I found out.
Day tripper, yeh.

110

"I can't get my winkle out
Isn't it a sin?
The more I try to get it out
The further it goes in!"

"You'd never believe the liberties the men take
down here. Perfect strangers too!"

"Oh, go on, Dick. The further
you're in the nicer it feels"

"I SUPPOSE YOU FIND THIS RATHER FLAT
AFTER THE ALPS, MR. MOUNTWELL?"

"KIDS HIMSELF HE'S A
GREAT LOVER—STARTS OFF WELL,
BUT CAN'T KEEP IT UP!"

Hello, Goodbye

You say yes, I say no,
You say stop, I say go, go, go.
Oh no.
You say goodbye and I say hello, hello,
hello.
I don't know why you say goodbye I say
hello, hello, hello.
I don't know why you say goodbye I say
hello.
I say high, you say low.
you say why and I say I don't know.
Oh no.
You say goodbye and I say hello, hello,
hello.
I don't know why you say goodbye I say
hello, hello, hello.
I don't know why you say goodbye I say
hello.
Why, why, why, why, why, why, do you
say goodbye, goodbye, bye, bye.
Oh no.
You say goodbye and I say hello, hello,
hello.
I don't know why you say goodbye I say
hello, hello, hello.
I don't know why you say goodbye I say
hello.
You say yes, I say no (I say yes but I may
mean no)
You say stop and I say go, go, go (I can
stay till it's time to go)
Oh, oh no.
You say goodbye and I say hello, hello,
hello.
I don't know why you say goodbye I say
hello, hello, hello.
I don't know why you say goodbye I say
hello, hello, hello.
I don't know why you say goodbye I say
hello, hello, hello.
hello, hello, hello.
Hela, heba, helloa.

''Those in the cheaper seats clap. The
rest of you rattle your jewellery.''
John, at the Royal Variety
Performance, November 15, 1963

Paperback writer

Paperback writer, Paperback writer.
Dear Sir or Madam will you read my
book,
It took me years to write will you take a
look,
Based on a novel by a man named Lear,
And I need a job,
So I want to be a paperback writer,
Paperback writer.
It's a dirty story of a dirty man,
And his clinging wife doesn't understand.
His son is working for the Daily Mail,
It's a steady job,
But he wants to be a paperback writer,
Paperback writer.
It's a thousand pages give or take a few,
I'll be writing more in a week or two,
I can make it longer if you like the style,
I can change it round,
And I want to be a paperback writer,
Paperback writer.
If you really like it you can have the
rights,
It could make a million for you overnight,
If you must return it you can send it here,
But I need a break,
And I want to be a paperback writer,
Paperback writer.

If I fell

If I fell in love with you would you
promise to be true,
And help me understand?
'Cos I've been in love before, and I found
that love was more,
Than just holding hands.
If I give my heart to you,
I must be sure from the very start,
That you would love me more than her.
If I trust in you, oh please,
Don't run and hide,
If I love you too, oh please don't hurt my
pride like her.
'Cos I couldn't stand the pain,
And I would be sad if our new love was in
vain.
So I hope you see,
That I would love to love you,
And that she will cry when she learns we
are two.
'Cos I couldn't stand the pain,
And I would be sad if our new love was
in vain.
So I hope you see,
That I would love to love you,
And that she will cry when she learns we
are two.
If I fell in love with you.

Paperback writer

Paperback writer, Paperback writer

Dear Sir or Madam will you read my book,
it took me years to write will you take a look,
based on a novel by a man named Lear,
and I need a job,
so I want to be a paperback writer,
paperback writer.

It's a dirty story of a dirty man,
and his clinging wife doesn't understand.
His son is working for the Daily Mail,
it's a steady job,
but he wants to be a paperback writer,
paperback writer.

It's a thousand pages give or take a few,
I'll be writing more in a week or two,
I can make it longer if you like the style,
I can change it round,
and I want to be a paperback writer,
paperback writer.

If you really like it you can have the rights,
it could make a million for you overnight,
if you must return it you can send it here,
but I need a break,
and I want to be a paperback writer,
paperback writer.

Paperback writer
"Everyone gets down on their knees and grovels a bit" – Paul

Think for yourself "It was just a beautiful idea of John's to plant an acorn, and the only way you can better John is by copying him exactly." – Yoko Ono

Think for yourself

I've got a word or two
to say about the things that you do,
you're telling all those lies,
about the good things that we can have if
we close our eyes.
Do what you want to do,
and go where you're going to,
think for yourself,
'cos I won't be there with you.
I left you far behind
the ruins of the life that you had in mind.
And though you still can't see,
I know your mind's made up, you're
gonna cause more misery.
Do what you want to do,
and go where you're going to,
think for yourself,
'cos I won't be there with you.
Although your mind's opaque,
try thinking more,
if just for your own sake.
the future still looks good,
and you've got time to rectify
all the things that you should.
Do what you want to do,
and go where you're going to,
think for yourself,
'cos I won't be there with you.
Do what you want to do,
and go where you're going to,
think for yourself,
'cos I won't be there with you.
Think for yourself,
'cos I won't be there with you.

You won't see me

When I call you up your line's engaged.
I have had enough, so act your age,
we have lost the time that was so hard to
find,
and I will lose my mind,
if you won't see me, you won't see me.
I don't know why you should want to
hide,
but I can't get through my hands are tied,
I won't want to stay I don't have much to
say,
but I can turn away,
and you won't see me, you won't see me.
Time after time you refuse to even listen,
I wouldn't mind if I knew what I was
missing.
Though the days are few they're filled
with tears,
and since I lost you it feels like years,
yes it seems so long girl since you've
been gone,
I just can't go on,
if you won't see me, you won't see me.
Time after time you refuse to even listen,
I wouldn't mind if I knew what I was
missing.
Though the days are few they're filled
with tears,
and since I lost you it feels like years,
yes it seems so long girl since you've
been gone,
I just can't go on,
if you won't see me, you won't see me.
Oo – Oo –

Yer blues

Yes I'm lonely wanna die
Yes I'm lonely wanna die.
If I ain't dead already.
Ooh girl you know the reason why.
In the morning wanna die.
In the evening wanna die.
If I ain't dead already.
Ooh girl you know the reason why.
My mother was of the sky.
My father was of the earth.
But I am of the universe
And you know what it's worth.
I'm lonely wanna die.
If I ain't dead already.
Ooh girl you know the reason why.
The eagle picks my eye.
The worm he licks my bone.
I feel so suicidal
Just like Dylan's Mr. Jones.
Lonely wanna die.
If I ain't dead already.
Ooh girl you know the reason why.
Black cloud crossed my mind.
Blue mist round my soul.
Feel so suicidal
Even hate my rock and roll.
Wanna die yeah wanna die.
If I ain't dead already.
Ooh girl you know the reason why.

"We're more popular than Jesus Christ now. I don't know which will go first. Rock and roll or Christianity. Jesus was all right, but his disciples were thick and ordinary. It's them twisting it that ruins it for me." – John

There's a place

There, there's a place,
Where I can go,
When I feel low,
When I feel blue,
And it's my mind,
And there's no time,
When I'm alone.
I think of you,
And things you do,
Go round my head,
The things you've said,
Like I love only you.
In my mind there's no sorrow,
Don't you know that it's so,
There'll be no sad tomorrow,
Don't you know that it's so.
There, there's a place,
Where I can go,
When I feel low,
When I feel blue,
And it's my mind,
And there's no time,
When I'm alone.
There, there's a place,
There's a place.

**"It was just like Butlins."
– Ringo, after returning
from meditating
at Rishikesh in the
Himalayas**

Tomorrow never knows

Turn off your mind relax and float
down-stream,
it is not dying, it is not dying,
lay down all thought surrender to the
void,
it is shining, it is shining.
That you may see the meaning of within,
it is speaking, it is speaking,
that love is all and love is ev'ryone,
it is knowing, it is knowing.
When ignorance and haste may mourn
the dead,
it is believing, it is believing.
But listen to the colour of your dreams,
it is not living, it is not living.
Or play the game existence to the end.
Of the beginning, of the beginning.
Of the beginning. Of the beginning.

**"Often the backing I think of early on
never comes off. With Tomorrow
Never Knows I'd imagined in my head
that in the background you would
hear thousands of monks chanting.
That was impractical of course and we
did something different. I should have
tried to get near my original idea, the
monks singing, I realise now that was
what it wanted." – John**

I'm looking through you

I'm looking through you, where did you
go?
I thought I knew you, what did I know?
You don't look different, but you have
changed,
I'm looking through you, you're not the
same.
Your lips are moving, I cannot hear,
your voice is soothing but the words
aren't clear.
You don't sound different, I've learnt
the game,
I'm looking through you, you're not the
same.
Why, tell me why did you not treat me
right?
Love has a nasty habit of disappearing
overnight,
you're thinking of me the same old way,
you were above me, but not today.
The only difference is you're down there.
I'm looking through you and you're
nowhere.
Why, tell me why did you not treat me
right?
Love has a nasty habit of disappearing
overnight,
I'm looking through you, where did you
go?
I thought I knew you, what did I know?
You don't look different, but you have
changed,
I'm looking through you, you're not the
same.
Yeh, I tell you you've changed.

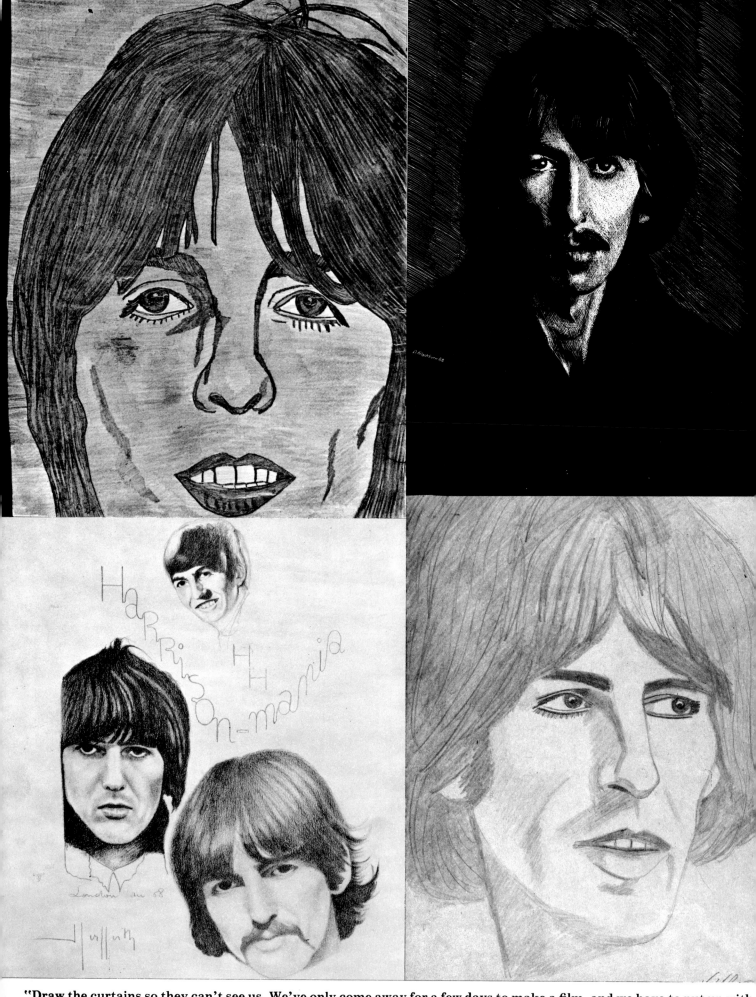

"**Draw the curtains so they can't see us. We've only come away for a few days to make a film, and we have to put up with**

'' – George, when fans laid seige to the hotel where the Beatles were staying during the filming of Magical Mystery Tour

Honey pie

She was a working girl
North of England way.
Now she's hit the big time
In the U.S.A.
And if she could only hear me
This is what I'd say.
Honey pie you are making me crazy.
I'm in love but I'm lazy.
So won't you please come home.
Oh honey pie my position is tragic.
Come and show me the magic
of your Hollywood Song.
You became a legend of the silver screen
And now the thought of meeting you
Makes me weak in the knee.
Oh honey pie you are driving me frantic.
Sail across the Atlantic
To be where you belong.
Will the wind that blew her boat
Across the sea
Kindly send her sailing back to me.
Honey pie you are making me crazy.
I'm in love but I'm lazy.
So won't you please come home.

**"I think people think I'm the cute
one." – Paul, on the David Frost
television show**

I want to hold your hand

Oh yeh, I'll tell you something,
I think you'll understand,
then I'll say that something,
I wanna hold your hand,
I wanna hold your hand,
I wanna hold your hand.
Oh please say to me
you'll let me be your man,
and please say to me
you'll let me hold your hand,
now let me hold your hand,
I wanna hold your hand.
And when I touch you
I feel happy inside,
it's such a feeling
that my love I can't hide,
I can't hide, I can't hide.
Yeh, you got that something,
I think you'll understand,
when I feel that something,
I wanna hold your hand,
I wanna hold your hand,
I wanna hold your hand.
And when I touch you
I feel happy inside,
it's such a feeling
that my love I can't hide,
I can't hide, I can't hide.
Yeh, you got that something,
I think you'll understand,
when I feel that something,
I wanna hold your hand,
I wanna hold your hand,
I wanna hold your hand.

**"The submediant switches from C
Major into A flat Major and to a lesser
extent mediant ones (e.g. I want to
hold your hand) are the trademark of
Lennon and McCartney songs." –
The Times Music Critic**

"I think it was Miss Daisy Hawkins originally – but I wanted a name that was more real. The thought just came: 'Eleanor Rigby picks up the rice and lives in a dream.' She didn't make it, she never made it with anyone, she didn't even look as if she was going to." – Paul

Eleanor Rigby

Ah, look at all the lonely people.
Ah, look at all the lonely people.
Eleanor Rigby picks up the rice in the church where a wedding has been,
lives in a dream.
Waits at the window, wearing the face that she keeps in a jar by the door,
Who is it for?
All the lonely people, where do they all come from?

All the lonely people, where do they all belong?
Father McKenzie, writing the words of a sermon that no-one will hear,
No-one comes near.
Look at him working, darning his socks in the night when there's nobody there,
What does he care?
All the lonely people, where do they all come from?
All the lonely people, where do they all belong?

Ah, look at all the lonely people.
Ah, look at all the lonely people.
Eleanor Rigby died in the church and was buried along with her name.
Nobody came.
Father McKenzie, wiping the dirt from his hands as he walks from the grave.
No-one was saved.
All the lonely people, where do they all come from?
All the lonely people, where do they all belong?

With a little help from my friends

What would you do if I sang out of tune,
would you stand up and walk out on me.
Lend me your ears and I'll sing you a
song,
and I'll try not to sing out of key.
I get by with a little help from my friends,
I get high with a little help from my
friends,
I'm gonna try with a little help from my
friends.
What do I do when my love is away.
(Does it worry you to be alone)
how do I feel by the end of the day
(are you sad because you're on your own)
no I get by with a little help from my
friends,
I get high with a little help from my
friends,
Oh I'm gonna try with a little help from
my friends.
Do you need anybody,
I need somebody to love.
Could it be anybody
I want somebody to love.
Would you believe in a love at first sight,
yes I'm certain that it happens all the
time.
What do you see when you turn out the
light,
I can't tell you, but I know it's mine.
Oh I get by with a little help from my
friends.
I get high with a little help from my
friends,
Oh I'm gonna try with a little help from
my friends.
Do you need anybody,
I just need somebody to love,
could it be anybody,
I want somebody to love. Oh
I get by with a little help from my friends,
Mm I'm gonna try with a little help from
my friends,
Oh I get high with a little help from my
friends,
Yes I get by with a little help from my
friends.

**"You know I'm not very good at
singing because I haven't got a great
range. So they write songs for me that
are pretty low and not too hard."** –
Ringo

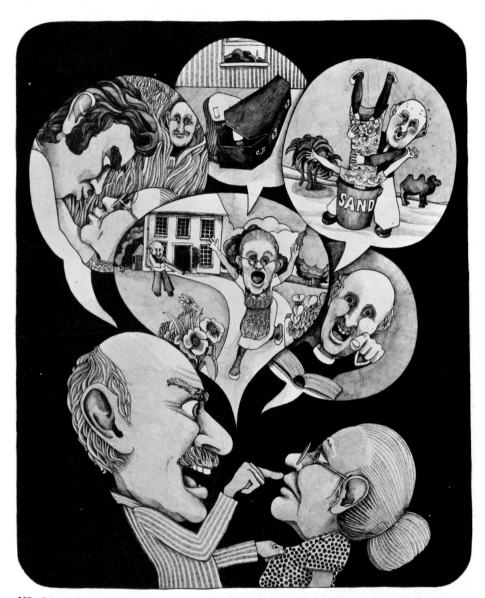

"I always hated 'Run for your life.' "—John

Run for your life

I'd rather see you dead, little girl,
than to be with another man.
You'd better keep your head, little girl,
or I won't know where I am.
You'd better run for your life
if you can, little girl,
hide your head in the sand, little girl.
Catch you with another man,
that's the end – ah, little girl.
Well you know that I'm a wicked guy,
and I was born with a jealous mind,
and I can't spend my whole life tryin',
just to make you toe the line.
You'd better run for your life
if you can, little girl,
hide your head in the sand, little girl,
catch you with another man,

that's the end – ah, little girl.
Let this be a sermon,
I mean everything I said,
baby, I'm determined,
and I'd rather see you dead.
You'd better run for your life
if you can, little girl,
hide your head in the sand, little girl,
catch you with another man,
that's the end – ah, little girl.
I'd rather see you dead, little girl,
than to be with another man,
you'd better keep your head, little girl,
or I won't know where I am.
You'd better run for your life,
if you can, little girl,
hide your head in the sand, little girl,
catch you with another man,
that's the end – ah, little girl.

LONDON: TEENAGE FANS SOB AT WEDDING OF
BEATLE PAUL McCARTNEY, MOST BELOVED MEM
FOURSOME, TO U.S. PHOTOGRAPHER LINDA EAS

MARRIED

FABULOUS

Baby's in black

Oh dear, what can I do?
Baby's in black and I'm feeling blue,
Tell me, oh what can I do?
She thinks of him and so she dresses in
black,
And though he'll never come back, she's
dressed in black.
Oh dear, what can I do?
Baby's in black and I'm feeling blue,
Tell me, oh what can I do?
I think of her, but she only thinks of him,
And though it's only a whim, she thinks
of him.
Oh how long will it take,
Till she sees the mistake she has made?
Dear what can I do?
Baby's in black and I'm feeling blue,
Tell me, oh what can I do?
Oh how long will it take,
Till she sees the mistake she has made?
Dear what can I do?
Baby's in black and I'm feeling blue,
Tell me, oh what can I do?
She thinks of him and so she dresses in
black,
And though he'll never come back, she's
dressed in black.
Oh dear, what can I do?
Baby's in black and I'm feeling blue,
Tell me, oh what can I do?

Your Mother should know

Let's all get up and dance to a song
that was a hit before your Mother was
born
Though she was born a long long time ag
your Mother should know – your Mother
should know
sing it again.
Lift up your hearts and sing me a song
that was a hit before your Mother was
born
Though she was born a long long time ag
your Mother should know – your Mother
should know
your Mother should know – your Mother
should know
sing it again.
Though she was born a long long time ag
your Mother should know – your Mother
should know
your Mother should know – your Mother
should know
your Mother should know – your Mother
should know.

Blue Jay Way

There's a fog upon L.A.
And my friends have lost their way
we'll be over soon they said
now they've lost themselves instead.
Please don't be long please don't you b
very long
please don't be long or I may be asleep
well it only goes to show
and I told them where to go
ask a policeman on the street
there's so many there to meet
please don't be long please don't you b
very long
please don't be long or I may be asleep
now it's past my bed I know
and I'd really like to go
soon will be the break of day
sitting here in Blue Jay Way
please don't be long please don't you b
very long
please don't be long or I may be asleep.
Please don't be long please don't you b
very long
please don't be long
please don't be long please don't you b
very long
please don't be long
please don't be long please don't you b
very long
please don't be long
don't be long – don't be long – don't be
long
don't be long – don't be long – don't be
long.

**"Derek got held up. He rang to say
he'd be late. I told him on the phone
that the house was in Blue Jay Way
He said he could find it okay, he cou
always ask a cop." – George**

Rain

If the rain comes they run and hide their heads,
They might as well be dead,
If the rain comes, if the rain comes.
When the sun shines they slip into the shade,
And sip their lemonade,
When the sun shines, when the sun shines.
Rain, I don't mind,
Shine, the weather's fine.
I can show you that when it starts to rain,
Everything's the same,
I can show you, I can show you.
Rain, I don't mind,
Shine, the weather's fine.
Can you hear me that when it rains and shines,
It's just a state of mind,
Can you hear me, can you hear me?

"On the end of 'Rain' you hear me singing it backwards. We'd done the main thing at EMI and the habit was then to take the song home and see what you thought a little extra gimmick or what the guitar piece would be. So I got home about five in the morning, stoned out of me head, I staggered up to me tape recorder and I put it on, but it came out backwards, and I was in a trance in the earphones, what is it, what is it. It's too much, you know, and I really wanted the whole song backwards almost, and that was it. So we tagged it on the end. I just happened to have the tape on the wrong way round, it just came out backwards, it just blew me mind. The voice sounds like an old Indian." – John, Rolling Stone

All you need is love

Love, love, love, love, love, love, love, love, love.
There's nothing you can do that can't be done.
Nothing you can sing that can't be sung.
Nothing you can say but you can learn how to play the game
It's easy.
There's nothing you can make that can't be made.
No one you can save that can't be saved.
Nothing you can do but you can learn how to be you in time
It's easy.
All you need is love, all you need is love,
All you need is love, love, love is all you need.
Love, love, love, love, love, love, love, love, love.
All you need is love, all you need is love,
All you need is love, love, love is all you need.
There's nothing you can know that isn't known.
Nothing you can see that isn't shown.
Nowhere you can be that isn't where you're meant to be.
It's easy.
All you need is love, all you need is love,
all you need is love, love, love is all you need.
All you need is love (all together now)
All you need is love (everybody)
All you need is love, love, love is all you need.

"We're going to send two acorns for peace to every world leader from John and Yoko. Perhaps if they plant them and watch them grow they may get the idea into their heads." – John

"Klaus (Voorman) had a harmonium in his house, which I hadn't played before. I was doodling on it, playing to amuse myself, when 'Within You' started to come. The tune came first then I got the first sentence. It came out of what we'd been doing that evening." – George

Within you without you

We were talking – about the space
between us all
And the people – who hide themselves
behind a wall of illusion
Never glimpse the truth – then it's far too
late – when they pass away.
We were talking – about the love we all
could share – when we find it
to try our best to hold it there – with our
love
With our love – we could save the world –
if they only knew.
Try to realise it's all within yourself
no-one else can make you change
And to see you're really only very small,
and life flows on within you and without
you.
We were talking – about the love that's
gone so cold and the people,
who gain the world and lose their soul –
they don't know – they can't see – are you
one of them?
When you've seen beyond yourself –
then you may find peace of mind, is
waiting there –
And the time will come when you see
we're all one,
and life flows on within you and without
you.

I want to tell you

I want to tell you,
my head is filled with things to say,
when you're here,
all those words they seem to slip away.
When I get near you,
the games begin to drag me down,
it's alright,
I'll make you maybe next time around.
But if I seem to act unkind,
it's only me, it's not my mind,
that is confusing things.
I want to tell you,
I feel hung up and I don't know why,
I don't mind, I could wait for ever,
I've got time.
Sometimes I wish I knew you well,
then I could speak my mind and tell you
may-be you'd understand.
I want to tell you,
I feel hung up and I don't know why,
I don't mind, I could wait for-ever,
I've got time. I've got time.

**"I mean we're human too. I do get
hurt when they attack Yoko or say
she's ugly or something." – John**

1. **When I'm sixty-four**
'You can knit a sweater by the fireside.'
2. **Yer blues**
'The eagle picks my eye. The worm he licks my bone.'
3. **The continuing story of Bungalow Bill**
'He went out tiger hunting with his elephant and gun
In case of accidents he always took his mom.'

4. **With a little help from my friends**
'Lend me your ears and I'll sing you a song.'
5. **Love you to**
'There's people standing round, who'll screw you in the ground.'
6. **Strawberry Fields forever**
7. **Lucy in the sky with diamonds**
'Picture yourself in a boat on a river . . . Cellophane

flowers of yellow and green, towering over your head.'
8. Sgt. Pepper's Lonely Hearts Club Band
  9. I am the walrus
'. . . they are the eggmen.'
10. Penny Lane
'. . . beneath the blue suburban skies.'

11. Glass onion
'Well here's another clue for you all the walrus was Paul.'
12. The fool on the hill
'But the fool on the hill sees the sun going down.'
13. Being for the benefit of Mr. Kite!
'. . . and of course Henry The Horse dances the waltz!'

139

Penny Lane

In Penny Lane there is a barber showing photographs
of ev'ry head he's had the pleasure to know.
And all the people that come and go
stop and say "Hello".
On the corner is a banker with a motorcar,
the little children laugh at him behind his back.
And the banker never wears a mac
In the pouring rain – very strange.
Penny Lane is in my ears and in my eyes,
there beneath the blue suburban skies
I sit, and meanwhile back
In Penny Lane there is a fireman with an hourglass
and in his pocket is a portrait of the Queen.
He likes to keep his fire engine clean,
it's a clean machine.
Penny Lane is in my ears and in my eyes,
a four of fish and finger pies
in summer meanwhile back
Behind the shelter in the middle of the round-a-bout
The pretty nurse is selling poppies from a tray.
And though she feels as if she's in a play
she is anyway.
In Penny Lane, the barber shaves another customer, we see the banker sitting waiting for a trim
and then the fireman rushes in
from the pouring rain – very strange.
Penny Lane is in my ears and in my eyes,
there beneath the blue suburban skies
I sit, and meanwhile back
Penny Lane is in my ears and in my eyes,
there beneath the blue suburban skies . . .
Penny Lane!

"Penny Lane is a bus roundabout in Liverpool; and there is a barber's shop showing photographs of every head he's had the pleasure to know – no that's not true, they're just photos of hairstyles, but all the people who come and go stop and say hello. It's part fact, part nostalgia for a place which is a great place, blue suburban skies as we remember it, and it's still there." – Paul

Birthday

You say it's your birthday.
It's my birthday too – yeah.
They say it's your birthday.
We're gonna have a good time.
I'm glad it's your birthday
Happy birthday to you.
Yes we're going to a party party
Yes we're going to a party party
Yes we're going to a party party.
I would like you to dance – Birthday
Take a cha-cha-cha-chance – Birthday
I would like you to dance – Birthday
dance
You say it's your birthday.
Well it's my birthday too – yeah.
You say it's your birthday.
We're gonna have a good time.
I'm glad it's your birthday
Happy birthday to you.

"I was 62 the day they had the premiere of 'Hard Day's Night' and we all went to the Dorchester. Then Paul handed me a big parcel – and I opened it and it was a picture of a horse. So I said 'Very nice' – but I thought, what do I want with a picture of a horse? Then Paul must have seen my face because he said 'It's not just a picture dad. I've bought you the bloody horse.' "—James McCartney

peter max

Lovely Rita

Lovely Rita meter maid.
Lovely Rita meter maid.
Lovely Rita meter maid.
Nothing can come between us,
when it gets dark I tow your heart away.
Standing by a parking meter,,
when I caught a glimpse of Rita,
filling in a ticket in her little white book.
In a cap she looked much older,
and the bag across her shoulder
made her look a little like a military man.
Lovely Rita meter maid,
may I inquire discreetly,
when you are free,
to take some tea with me.
Took her out and tried to win her,
had a laugh and over dinner,
told her I would really like to see her
again,
got the bill and Rita paid it,
took her home and nearly made it,
sitting on a sofa with a sister or two.
Oh, lovely Rita meter maid,
where would I be without you.
give us a wink and make me think of you.

**"I was bopping about on the piano in
Liverpool when someone told me that
in America they call parking-meter
women meter-maids. I thought that
was great and it got to be Rita Meter
Maid and then Lovely Rita Meter Maid
and I was thinking that it should be a
hate song . . . but then I thought it
would be better to love her, and if she
was very freaky too, like a military
man, with a bag on her shoulder. A
foot stomper, but nice." – Paul**

Glass onion

I told you about strawberry fields.
You know the place where nothing is
real.
Well here's another place you can go
Where everything flows.
Looking through the bent backed tulips
To see how the other half live
Looking through a glass onion.
I told you about the walrus and me – man.
You know that we're as close as can be –
man.
Well here's another clue for you all
The walrus was Paul.
Standing on the cast iron shore – yeah.
Lady Madonna trying to make ends meet
– yeah.
Looking through a glass onion.
Oh yeah oh yeah oh yeah
Looking through a glass onion.
I told you about the fool on the hill.
I tell you man he living there still.
Well here's another place you can be.
Listen to me.
Fixing a hole in the ocean
Trying to make a dove-tail joint – yeah
Looking through a glass onion.

Get back

(1)
Jojo was a man who thought he was a
loner
But he knew it couldn't last.
Jojo left his home in Tucsan, Arizona
For some California Grass.
Get back, get back.
Get back to where you once belonged
Get back, get back.
Get back to where you once belonged.
Get back Jojo. Go home
Get back, get back.
Back to where you once belonged
Get back, get back.
Back to where you once belonged.
Get back Jo.
(2)
Sweet Loretta Martin thought she was a
woman
But she was another man
All the girls around her say she's got it
coming
But she gets it while she can.
Get back, get back.
Get back to where you once belonged
Get back, get back
Get back to where you once belonged.
Get back Loretta. Go home
Get back, get back.
Get back to where you once belonged
Get back, get back.
Get back to where you once belonged.
Get back Loretta
Your mother's waiting for you
Wearing her high-heel shoes
And her low-neck sweater
Get on home Loretta
Get back, get back.
Get back to where you once belonged.

Get back "We were sitting in the
studio and we made it up out of thin
air . . . we started to write words there
and then . . . when we finished it, we
recorded it at Apple Studios and made
it into a song to roller-coast by." – Paul

145

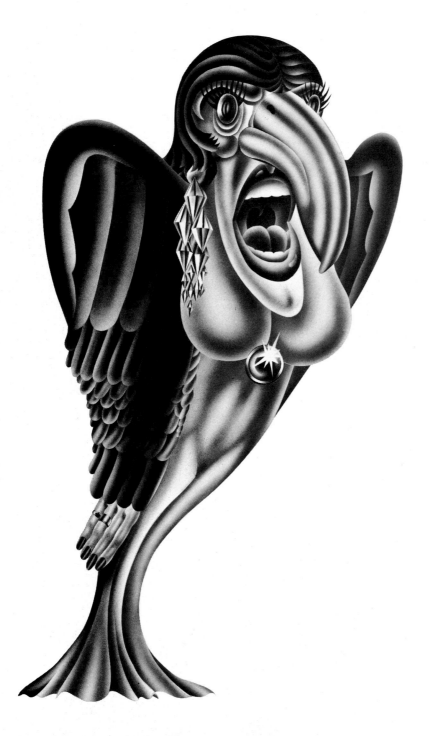

And your bird can sing

You tell me that you've ev'ry thing you want,
And your bird can sing,
But you don't get me,   You don't get me.
You say you've seen seven wonders,
And your bird is green,
But you can't see me,   You can't see me.
When your prized possessions start to wear you down,
Look in my direction I'll be round,
I'll be round.
When your bird is broken will it bring you down?
You may be awoken I'll be round,
I'll be round.
Tell me that you've heard ev'ry sound there is,
And your bird can swing,
But you can't hear me,
You can't hear me.

Dear Prudence

Dear Prudence, won't you come out to play.
Dear Prudence, greet the brand new day.
The sun is up, the sky is blue.
It's beautiful and so are you.
Dear Prudence won't you come out to play?
Dear Prudence open up your eyes.
Dear Prudence see the sunny skies.
The wind is low the birds will sing
That you are part of everything.
Dear Prudence won't you open up your eyes?
Look around round
Look around round round
Look around.
Dear Prudence let me see you smile.
Dear Prudence like a little child.
The clouds will be a daisy chain.
So let me see you smile again.
Dear Prudence won't you let me see you smile?

Hey bulldog

Sheep dog standing in the rain.
Bull frog doing it again.
Some kind of happiness is measured out in
miles.
What makes you think you're something
special when you smile.
Child-like yeah, no one understands.
Jack-knife in your sweaty hands.
Some kind of innocence is measured out
in years.
You don't know what it's like to listen to
your fears.
You can talk to me,
You can talk to me,
You can talk to me,
If you're lonely you can talk to me (yeah!)
Big man walking in the park
Wigwam frightened of the dark
Some kind of solitude is measured out in
you.
You think you know it but you haven't
got a clue.
You can talk to me,
You can talk to me,
You can talk to me,
If you're lonely you can talk to me (yeah!)
Hey bulldog, hey bulldog, hey bulldog
Hey, Bulldog, Woof!
wha'd'ya say?
I said woof!
d'y' know any more?·
Wowu-wa Ah!

**"Paul said we should do a real song in
the studio, to save wasting time.
Could I whip one off? I had a few
words at home so I brought them in." –
John, on how 'Hey bulldog' was
recorded**

It's all too much

It's all too much
It's all too much
When I look into your eyes
Your love is there for me
And the more I go inside
The more there is to see.
It's all too much for me to take
The love that's shining all around you
Everywhere it's what you make
for us to take it's all too much.
Floating down the stream of time
From life to life with me
Makes no difference where you are
or where you'd like to be.
It's all too much for me to take
The love that's shining all around here.
All the world is birthday cake
so take a piece but not too much.
Sail me on a silver sun
Where I know that I am free
Show me that I'm everywhere
and get me home for tea.
It's all too much for me to take
There's plenty there for everybody
The more you give the more you get
The more it is and it's too much.
It's all too much for me to see
The love that's shining all around you
The more I learn the less I know
But what I do is all too much.
It's all too much for me to take
The love that's shining all around you
Everywhere it's what you make
for us to take it's all too much.
It's much, it's much.
It's too much
Ah! it's too much
You are too much ah!
We are dead ah!
Too much, too much, too much-a. FADE

**"George is turning out songs like Soft
Mick these days." – John**

All Together Now

One, two, three, four,
Can I have a little more,
Five, six, seven, eight, nine, ten,
I love you.
A, B, C, D,
Can I bring my friend to tea,
E, F, G, H, I, J,
I love you.
Bom bom bom bom-pa bom
Sail the ship bom-pa bom
Chop the tree bom-pa bom
Skip the rope bom-pa bom
Look at me.
All together now, All together now,
All together now, All together now.
Black, white, green, red,
Can I take my friend to bed,
Pink, brown, yellow, orange and blue,
I love you.
All together now, All together now,
All together now, All together now,
Bom bom bom bom bom-pa bom
Sail the ship bom-pa bom
Chop the tree bom-pa bom
Skip the rope bom-pa bom
Look at me
All together now, All together now,
All together now, All together now,
All together now!

**"The thing is, we're all really the
same person. We're just four parts of
the one." – Paul**

P.S. I love you

As I write this letter, send my love to you
remember that I'll always be in love with
you.
Treasure these few words till we're
together
keep all my love forever.
P.S. I love you, you, you, you.
I'll be coming home again to you love,
until the day I do love.
P.S. I love you, you, you, you.
As I write this letter, send my love to you
remember that I'll always be in love with
you.
Treasure these few words till we're
together
keep all my love forever.
P.S. I love you, you, you, you.
As I write this letter, send my love to you
(you know I want you to)
remember that I'll always be in love with
you.
I'll be coming home again to you love,
until the day I do love.
P.S. I love you, you, you, you.
I love you.

P.S. I love you
**"I didn't really feel I belonged
until after the first two years,
maybe two and a half. You know,
before it was them, the Beatles
and me – the new drummer.
It lasted long enough to bother a bit
but not any more." – Ringo**

''The copper came to the door, to tell
us about the accident. It was just like
it's supposed to be, the way it is in the
films. Asking if I was her son, and all
that. Then he told us, and we both
went white. It was the worst thing that
ever happened to me.'' – John

Julia

Half of what I say is meaningless
But I say it just to reach you, Julia.
Julia, Julia, oceanchild, calls me
So I sing a song of love, Julia
Julia, seashell eyes, windy smile, calls me

So I sing a song of love, Julia.
Her hair of floating sky is shimmering,
glimmering,
In the sun.
Julia, Julia, morning moon, touch me
So I sing a song of love, Julia.
When I cannot sing my heart

I can only speak my mind, Julia.
Julia, sleeping sand, silent cloud, touch
me
So I sing a song of love, Julia.
Hum hum hum hum . . . calls me
So I sing a song of love for Julia, Julia,
Julia.

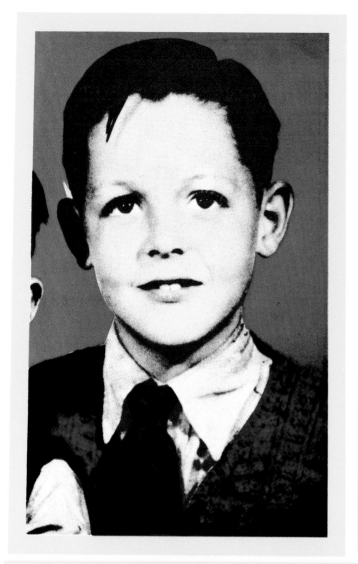

Index

Acknowledgements

This book could not have been compiled without a great deal of help. Because of space, it is not possible to mention everyone by name, but we should like to express our thanks to all the people who took part in its production, particularly Art Kane, who started the ball rolling, and the contributors who produced pictures for little reward. We are also indebted to the fans whose response to our ads was astonishing: Ken White, Thelma Cowen, Alan Birch, Allan Jones, Frances Platt, G. Dean, Molly Booth, David Wright, Anita Johnson, Carole Smith, Tony Rushton, Doreen Hyde, Joan Langford, Richard Phillips, Shennell Rothman, Terry Hynes, Hilary Petch, Dennis McKeown, Irene Hanson, B. Cawson, L. Baker, Martin Lawson, Stephen McGee, Joanne Thomson, F. Ashcroft, Christine and Pauline Westley, S. McCarthy, Pat Laythorpe, Alan Crawley, Stewart Emmott, S. Hurst, V. McCartney, C. Hanne, P. Stennet, Jan Moller, B. Cohen, Allan Le Carpentier, K. Voels, Kevin Day, Mike Davies, Alan Platt and many others whom we have forgotten. Special assistance in the design of the book was provided by David Hillman and Gilvrie Misstear, and Bob Smithers, James Marsh and Harry Willock sweated through many sleepless nights building models and spraying colours. We should also like to thank Ray Connolly, who prepared the captions.

We should like to thank Heinemann for giving us their kind permission to publish extracts from THE BEATLES: the authorised biography by Hunter Davies.

Alan Aldridge left school when he was 15, then drifted through a multiplicity of jobs. He was an insurance clerk, a barrow boy and an actor in repertory. When he was 20 he started to draw. That was in 1963. Today he is one of the great original forces at work in the world of creative graphics. His style is distinctive and immediate, fantasy with a hard edge. His design and use of colour has inspired many imitators, none of whom has yet matched his own idiosyncratic vision. He has won many design awards, including a silver medal from the Designers and Art Directors Association and The Scotsman International Design Award twice, and his work is a familiar feature of Britain's magazines, advertisement billboards and record covers. His interest in the comic strip form led to his earlier work 'The Penguin Book of Comics' which he produced with George Perry.